Praise for
MIXED-UP LOVE

"Reflects on the new frontiers of interfaith marriage, and publishing veteran Sweeney can be depended on to know what makes a good book." —*Publishers Weekly*

"We're way beyond Christmas and Hanukkah here. Sweeney and Woll offer a moving, personal reflection on their search for the divine in everyday life. *Mixed-Up Love* is an instructive, refreshing, and spiritually sophisticated guide for any couple seeking to navigate a complex religious path."
—Rabbi Lawrence Kushner, Emanu-El Scholar at Congregation Emanu-El of San Francisco and the author of *Kabbalah: A Love Story*

"What unites us is so much greater than what separates us. If we're sometimes mixed-up, this book can help sort it out."
—Lama Surya Das, author of *Awakening the Buddha Within: Tibetan Wisdom for the Western World*, and founder of the Dzogchen Center in America

"One of the most moving and candid love stories I have ever read...mature, sure of itself, deft in its telling, rich in its sharing. Whether you are interested in the possibilities and intricacies of interfaith marriage or not, you are going to be grateful that Sweeney and Woll are and that they have been willing to tell the rest of us why."
—Phyllis Tickle, compiler, *The Divine Hours*

"Jon and Michal take us into the most intimate space of all, an interfaith marriage, and provide millions of similar couples with light and warmth on the complicated path of committing to faith and one another when the faiths are different. This is a generous and important book."

—Eboo Patel, author of *Acts of Faith* and *Sacred Ground*

"Jon Sweeney and Michal Woll have written an extremely important book for our era, and they have done so with depth, integrity, and humor. The book is beautifully written, and the back and forth dialogue between this husband and wife makes for exciting reading. Maybe their love is not so 'mixed-up' after all."

—Rabbi David Zaslow, author of *Jesus: First Century Rabbi*

"All of us are figuring out how to be one big human family on one small planet—when members of our family follow many different religions. Jon and Michal are figuring out how that works in one household, and they share both their experience and the wisdom they've gained through it in this charming, enjoyable, and insightful book."

—Brian D. McLaren, author/speaker/activist (brianmclaren.net)

"Jon Sweeney and Michal Woll represent a new kind of American family, one that celebrates and learns from difference. Readers, in turn, will celebrate and learn from this book about their experiences together, whether it's planning a wedding or dealing with 'the December dilemma.'"

—Jana Riess, author of *Flunking Sainthood* and the Twible

"Woll and Sweeney raise important questions in an engagingly frank way for all interfaith couples.... They also add to the growing and multi-faceted conversation about rabbis with non-Jewish partners."

—Rabbi Ellen Lippmann

MIXED-UP LOVE

RELATIONSHIPS, FAMILY, *and*
RELIGIOUS IDENTITY
in the 21ST CENTURY

JON M. SWEENEY *and* **MICHAL WOLL**

JERICHO
BOOKS

New York   Boston   Nashville

Out of a desire for privacy, brevity, clarity, or due to the faulty memory of the authors, some characters are composites and some names, personal details, and event sequences have been modified.

Unless otherwise noted, scripture quotations are from the New Revised Standard Version Bible, copyright © 1989 National Council of the Churches of Christ in the United States of America. Used by permission.
All rights reserved.

The authors are represented by Daniel Literary Group, Nashville, TN.

Jericho Books
Hachette Book Group
237 Park Avenue
New York, NY 10017

www.JerichoBooks.com

Printed in the United States of America

RRD-C

First Edition: October 2013

10 9 8 7 6 5 4 3 2 1

Jericho Books is an imprint of Hachette Book Group, Inc.
The Jericho Books name and logo are trademarks of
Hachette Book Group, Inc.

The Hachette Speakers Bureau provides a wide range of authors for speaking events. To find out more, go to www.HachetteSpeakersBureau.com or call (866) 376-6591.

The publisher is not responsible for websites (or their content) that are not owned by the publisher.

Library of Congress Control Number: 2013941775
ISBN: 978-1-4555-4589-6 (pbk.)

To Susie Learmonth and Jane Curtis,
dear friends and matriarchs,
who have always embraced us both individually
and together

Contents

Contents

PART IV
Re-creating the Future

MIXED-UP LOVE

PREFACE

As we approached the project of writing a book prompted by our lives and stories, we were immediately faced with the *how* of it. We, Michal and Jon, are writing this book together, but also separately. The lessons we are learning, or attempting to learn, are often similar and sometimes the same, but not always or entirely. The nature of this book, and of our stories, which begin in such different places, urges each of us to fully express our thoughts and experiences before we consider our shared ideas or outlook. **And so there are times when we are writing alone, either as Michal or Jon, and the text will appear in this typeface with our names at the beginning for clarity.** When you see this typeface, we are speaking in one voice. When writing alone we are often sharing parts of our personal stories, but we also take these opportunities to bring our perspectives and opinions, as well as Michal's professional experiences.

We are not experts. We are living this and continually figuring it out and we want to help others do the same. Our experiences are mostly in Judaism and Christianity. Today, about 2 percent of North Americans identify as Jewish, 75 percent as some sort of Christian, and 20 percent as "nones"—self-described as without any formal religious identification. If you do the math, that's most of us. But regardless of your own background, identification, or practice, we believe that the issues and examples we share, the questions and concerns we raise, will feel relevant to your situation and your experience.

We all have our unique journeys to take, and each of ours is both similar to and surely different from your own. Yet, if you are part of an interfaith couple of any constellation, we are confident that you will see some signposts from your own pathway in the world as you "look in" on ours. Or if you are someone interested in understanding religious life, who believes that all of our diverse paths can support, or empower, or bolster divine work in the world, you are welcome here.

Thanks for making us a part of your journey.

Unequally Yoked?

MICHAL It happens all the time, whether I am discussing my family constellation or making an introduction. But I often don't realize it's happening until the spelling actually starts.

"My husband is Jon, J-O-N. As in Jonathan." Somehow, clarifying that Jon isn't a J-O-H-N seems to soften the coming blow, at least for me. I hate to admit that I only discovered Jon's full name some months after our courtship had begun and that, yes, I was more comfortable that he wasn't a John.

I never actually spell Sweeney, since it is clearly so far away from Levine or Goldstein. Why bother? That is, unless I am trying to convince the customer service rep from the phone company to speak directly to me, in which case I am more likely spelling M-I-C-H-A-L while trying to explain to them that there *is no* Michael at our house; I am *not* Michael's wife; and I *am* a registered customer on the account! But that's an entirely different story. As it happens, I graduated from rabbinical school with a Rabbi Megan Doherty, and the very first bar mitzvah in the history of the synagogue I served in

Woodstock, Vermont, was named Sam McWilliams. So, a lovely Irish name doesn't necessarily prove anything.

Of course, because I am a rabbi, people often assume that Jon has converted to Judaism, which would make the entire name issue irrelevant. But instead, they have to assimilate the information that Rabbi Michal is married to Sweeney, John or no John.

The funny part of all the name stuff is that Jon has always seemed to me to be more connected to his Italian roots than the Irish, whose name he bears. Way back when, the family name was San Romani, and I have heard many stories of the past generations, including his rogue cousin Achilles. I have often joked that our daughter's full name is Sima Aleeza San Romani Woll, and I like to sing this name to the tune of one of our favorite Shabbat melodies, most often used for Psalm 121. Yes, that's S-I-M-A. It means treasure, a joyful treasure. And she is one.

JON It happens all the time. The real trouble begins at about the sixth line of dialogue:

"How are you doing, Jon? Great to see you! What are you up to?"

"Good. I'm good. Really good, in fact."

"I heard that you became a Catholic, and got married—and, wow... you've lost a lot of weight!"

"Yeah, that's true. How are you?" But, polite as they are, they doggedly stay on me and my changes... no luck changing the subject. Sometimes, Michal is standing beside me, in which case there is also a toddler in one of our pairs of arms at that moment, and their eyes clearly shift in her direction.

"Yes, that's right. This is my wife, Michal Woll." They greet. Hello. Hello. Smiles all around. Nice to meet you.

"And this is our daughter, Sima," I explain.

Oh, she's so cute. So precious. What beautiful eyes. And those thighs! Yes. Yes. Smile.

"Sima...how do you spell that? It's unusual."

"S-I-M-A. It was her great-grandmother's name. It's Hebrew. It means 'treasure.' "

Then, they ask meekly if what they heard is true. Looking at Michal. "And did I hear that you are a rabbi?"

"Yes, I am...a Reconstructionist," Michal replies simply, still smiling. And then, since this is one of my people, Michal looks to me like a circus performer who has just done something relatively simple on the floor, and I'm about to attempt something in the air.

"Yes," I boldly begin [too boldly?], "that's right..."

"How does that work for you, Jon?" There is a clear look of concern. You see, this person can ask me such a sensitive never-ask-religious question. We've known each other for a long time. We know all about each other and our whole religious milieu.

"Well, as you know, I am a Catholic, although not a very good one." I see a smirk arising. "My [do I sound defensive?] primary spiritual practice these days is actually Jewish." The facial contortions usually begin about here. "Michal and I keep a Jewish home. And we are raising Sima as a Jew."

My friend or colleague, who "knows" all about me and my background, now has a look of worry and confusion that causes him or her to resemble one of those faces in a Picasso painting.

I try to joke: "I'm like Saint Peter...right?"

☾ 卍 ☯ ✡ ☌ ☮

It happens all the time. People meet, fall in love, get married. Just a few generations ago, you would likely have married someone down the block, or a friend of the family, maybe even your second cousin. Very likely this someone would be one of "your people," someone who looked and thought a lot like you. A generation before that, your life partner might have been selected by your parents, and of course this still is the case in some places and cultures.

Once upon a time we lived much more segregated lives—when a Presbyterian dating a Baptist, not to mention a Catholic marrying a Jew, might upset not only a family, but an entire neighborhood.

We both grew up in the Chicago suburbs in the 1970s. In Skokie, Michal remembers fondly two special girlfriends in her junior high; both blondes named Maria, they went to catechism instead of Hebrew school on Wednesday afternoons. How exotic they were! And there was only one black boy in her class prior to entering high school. Meanwhile, in Wheaton, Jon cannot recall ever meeting a Jewish child in school, but does sheepishly admit to teasing the Catholic kids on the school bus, convinced by the teachings of his church that they were definitely wrong and probably doomed to hell. But times and people have changed. Society is more integrated, at least relative to race and religion. Within two decades, Michal's elementary school could no longer justify closing for the Jewish holidays. Jon fell in love with the Catholic tradition he was taught to shun.

Religion is simply not the great organizer it once was. Spirituality, often disconnected from organized religion, has been on the rise for a while, and religious identity is more fluid than ever before. Exposure and access to multiple faith traditions creates opportunity for experimentation and multiplicity. Your religious identity can be hyphenated; or you can just as easily have none at all. Independent and alternative forms and sites of worship are emerging as traditional institutions and practice wanes. People who do choose to pray with a congregation might walk to a nearby home or travel far from their parish to pray at a church matching their values. These categories did not exist when we were in high school, or if they did, they certainly didn't appear on any surveys of religious life.

Cultural divides have been replaced to some extent by divisions according to education level, professional status, and economics. At university, you can fall in love with someone from around the world. With men and women participating more equally at work, and work becoming a more encompassing aspect of contemporary life, the workplace is as likely a place to meet your spouse as your neighborhood pub or your church. And then, of course, there is the Internet, which has changed the whole concept of what it even means to "meet."

In the 21st century, religion is only one of myriad labels young people might choose to use to identify themselves, if they choose any at all. Labels and differentiation seem to have much less value in our culture than they once did. In a world where even gender has lost the sense of binary, many traditional categories are now fluid, or simply absent. Couples are rarely using religion as a litmus test for whom to marry, compared to previous generations. For example, a 2007 survey of young Catholics done by the Center for Applied Research in the Apostolate at Georgetown University found that, among those who had never married, only 7 percent responded that it was "very important" to wed someone who was also Catholic.[1] Meanwhile, people often recoil from words like "interfaith" and are less and less interested in qualifying at all who they love and who, or if, they marry. Previous generations could not have imagined such things.

Intermarriage is far from new and is growing steadily in this novel world where the boundaries between people are porous as they have never been before and religious difference is no longer threatening. For example, nearly one-third of all currently married Jews are intermarried and at least half of the Jews getting married today will marry a non-Jew. And intermarried Christians, according to the General Social Survey, are just as common and show the same trend. In total, 15 percent of all American households represented mixed faith in 1988. By 2006 this percentage increased to 25 percent. Recent surveys of young people in the Dharmic (Hindu, Jain, Sikh, Buddhist) and Muslim communities suggest similar trends, resulting in current intermarriage rates between 38 and 45 percent. All of this means there are at least 12 million more interfaith households in the United States than there were only a short while ago.

We met in Vermont, to where we each had moved for jobs years earlier. Both Chicagoans, we were separately but equally far from home. Introduced by a common friend, we were similar in age and had had similar experiences: college, grad school, careers, and prior relationships that had failed. We didn't share one of those things that spouses were supposed to have in common, for one of us was a Jew, the other a Christian.

But our religious lives, which were seen as such a fatal

difference, were actually something that drew us together. We both loved scripture, religious practice, and theology, and God and religion were part of our daily lives. Our religious approaches and commitments were well aligned and created in each of us values that we shared.

Still, when our story unfolds we find that others are surprised and we sometimes go on the defensive. Perhaps this is because we are not millennials imbedded in a culture that thinks in more conventional terms. We're both in our upper forties. Perhaps because we have not disposed of our labels or shunned our traditions but have instead embraced each other and are creating a life together. Perhaps because while we are highly engaged with religious thought and practice, we have stepped out of line with the classic mindsets of our Christian or Jewish counterparts.

We discovered early on that Christian and Jewish tendencies and concerns are different, and that we tend to shy away from both. For example, for those close to the world of Jon's upbringing the looming question often is, "But what do you *believe*?" As you will learn, Jon does not find this question, or any potential answer, to be a good barometer of his religious or spiritual life. On the other hand, many in the Jewish world could hardly care less what you believe as long as you *count*. Jewish identity and Jewish population are practically obsessions in the Jewish world. But as Michal explains, genetic Judaism is not very interesting to her.

Some of the common reactions to, and assumptions about, our marriage come directly from these conventional models. Does intermarriage pose the greatest challenge to the future of Judaism since the Holocaust? Is the choice to marry a non-Christian a dangerous symptom of a faith that no longer means anything? We don't think so.

So what is left in an era where belief is not essential for religious identity, or a world where religious identity is not necessary at all? What else do we need at a time when religious identity alone is insufficient for a rich spiritual life? Our answer is practice. At home, in community, on your own, with others, in prayer, through study or service, practice seems to be the essence of our spiritual life and the glue that holds our relationship, home, and our communities together.

In a traditional Christian context we would be called "unequally yoked." The apostle Paul wrote in Second Corinthians: "Be not unequally yoked together with unbelievers," according to the King James version of the Bible. More recent translations often render "unequally yoked" as "mismatched." Knowledgeable Jew that he was, Paul surely got this idea from the Torah, where Deuteronomy 22 offers three specific instructions. "You shall not sow your vineyard with a second kind of seed," it says, "or the whole yield will have to be forfeited, both the crop that you have sown and the yield of the vineyard itself." "You shall not plow with an ox and a donkey yoked together." And, "You shall not wear clothes made of wool and linen woven together." While the original intent and extent of Paul's turn of phrase is unclear, Christians and others have subsequently used "unequally yoked" over the centuries to justify or explain why people of different backgrounds, races, religions, and denominations should not be brought together, in marriage or even in community or in friendship.

When we first discussed sharing the story of our marriage

as a book project, Wendy Grisham, our publisher, mentioned that New Testament phrase, "unequally yoked." Michal did not have a context for it. She could immediately identify the biblical commandment against yoking together animals of unequal strength or size in order to protect the animals' safety, but her primary understanding of "yoke" was from the rabbinic literature and liturgy. There, *ol malchut shamayim*, or "the yoke of the kingship of heaven," describes the desirable life, one that is committed to following God's commandments, the divine intention for the world. The daily liturgy describes angels who "receive upon themselves, from each to each, the yoke of heaven's rule, and lovingly [they] give to one another the permission to declare their maker holy." This is—intentionally and perhaps ironically—the life that we strive to create for ourselves, our family, our community.

On a recent Friday evening before Shabbat dinner, as we stood in the kitchen with some friends we described our book to them and explained the idea of "unequally yoked." When that metaphor didn't register, we asked for advice on a title. Our friend Jay thought for a moment, then quickly said: " 'You are dead to me.' Well, that's what my parents would've called it!" Jay was mostly kidding, but his suggestion echoed a stereotypical Jewish response. It is true that what some Christians may have once called "unequally yoked" is what some Jews would have regarded as a kind of death: to family, to tradition, to peoplehood, should their Jewish child wed a non-Jew. There are even parents who would actually sit *shiva* for a child who "married out."[2]

The Talmud often addresses situations by imagining the most extreme of examples, examples whose conclusions might help to create definitions and boundaries. For example, in explaining how to stand and say the *Amidah*, the central prayer of the daily services, there are some basic guidelines. But what if you are traveling? Or if you are traveling and can't get off your donkey? What if you happen to be on a boat? Or in a place filled with beasts or robbers? *Then*, how should you say your prayer (Babylonian Talmud *Berachot* 28b)? There are ways in which we, as a couple, too feel like we might play that role, representing the boundaries of what is and is not possible in the ways of love and family. But there is no denying the presence and increasing frequency of interfaith relationships, so arguing with them can seem like disputing the tide schedule and analyzing them feels like describing life in a fish tank while standing thirty feet away. But we cannot claim that our relationship has been easy. Nor should it be. There are still many issues to be worked out between couples of different religious backgrounds, if it's going to work.

So, are we unusual? Not by a long shot. As the world becomes smaller and as many different religious or non-religious people come to live in community together, there are interfaith or non-faith couples of all sorts. For example, there is the relationship in which neither partner is particularly religious, at least when they meet as single adults. Yet the immediate need to create a suitable wedding ceremony, which usually involves family and tradition, brings religion quickly from the background to the fore, at least temporarily. And the arrival of children does the same. Many a couple has not participated in a religious ritual since their wedding day or the birth of their last child.

It is also common to find couples in which one partner is connected to a distinctive tradition while the other is atheist, agnostic, disinterested, or even hostile, sometimes due to negative experiences in his or her own religious background. And then, of course, a full 20 percent of North Americans are now self-defined nones, checking the "none" box when asked for a religious affiliation. Each of these constellations provides its own set of challenges. Some couples may have it easier than we do; others may find their differences to be more of a struggle. You will learn more in the chapters that follow.

Plenty of books have been published that discuss interfaith relationships and marriage.[3] Most are written by academics or religious professionals and based on research and surveys that point to an alarming cultural trend. They are full of statistics, case studies, and anecdotes from dozens of couples, as well as insights from clergy and relationship experts from all sorts of backgrounds.

We suspect, however, that these books mostly sit lonely on library shelves and very few people who are not professionally involved in some way read them. Why? Because by their very nature these studies lack the nuance and richness of real lives and firsthand experience that those of us involved in interfaith relationships need in order to relate to the topic in a personal way. Myriad examples of couples and their choices have made it clear that there are countless ways to deal with your wedding, your children, and your religious practices within or beyond your home. Whatever you envision for your family, rest assured it has been done before, perhaps by Joan and Ken in Cleveland.

We hope to do something different. We are animating the discussions of where society is at present, where it is going, what decisions face an interfaith couple, and what it all means, with our own life experiences. And we integrate our story of religious difference within the fullness of two complex lives, of which religion is still only a part. We share our passions and fears, our dedication and insecurities, the questions we have asked and are still asking, and occasionally we offer answers. Yes, one of us is Jewish and a rabbi. One of us is Catholic and works in Christian publishing. But that does not tell our story *in toto*, nor the stories of the other couples and families who appear in this book.

Mixed-Up Love addresses the challenges, compromises, and thoughtfulness that are inherent to creating homes and communities that are full of love and spirit in all of its forms. We write for intermarried couples and families who seek to create meaningful spiritual and religious lives in a time when belief is no longer what defines religious identity and yet the distinctiveness of religious traditions still matters. We write so that you might ask, and keep asking, the questions that will lead you along your path toward a life that fulfills your own yearnings for richness and meaning within a loving relationship.

In today's parlance we are an interfaith couple, but that is not what we feel like with each other. A relatively new category of religious life, "interfaith" is neither appealing nor describes us very well; something about the word feels unsure, unstable. We really are none of those things. We are not a Jew and a Christian, separated religiously, united in marriage. Instead, we share a life infused with religious thought, spiritual practice, and personal choices based on shared values that stem from our belief in a God that works in the world. We believe that we are, to put it quite simply, and despite how it may look from the outside, equally yoked.

PART I

Becoming Ourselves

Some of us grow up sitting next to our parents in the pews and stay there throughout our lives. Others rarely see a pew, and still others reach an age of independence, lose interest in our childhood faith, and perhaps move on to something new. We can spend a lifetime figuring out who we are and what we do or do not believe.

Experiences, choices, and lessons learned over decades create the people we are and the stories we bring to our coupled lives. Imagining a life together makes little sense without first trying to understand the stories of our lives apart.

And while we are forging our paths, the religious land-scape is shifting, creating new forms of practice and com-munity and shunning labels and assumptions about what it means to be a person with faith.

———

CHAPTER 1

Leaving Home

We love to go hiking in state parks. Along mountain paths there are signs, similar to most roadways, telling you what to expect and how to stay on the path. Someone has usually hashed marks of paint on trees, a small swath of white or yellow on the bark, showing the best way to progress upward. There can be so many hashes and signs by journey's end, it feels like cheating to say you actually hiked a mountain. Such a hike can seem less like an adventurous journey than like falling forward in the way you're pointed. This is not what explorers were doing when they sought the source of the Nile.

Such clear signage isn't usually available in life, personal, professional, or religious. But it sounds a bit like how Jon's Sunday school teachers who used to speak of "following God's will," which was supposed to be easily discernible from reading the Bible. Surely, it's never that simple. Or at least it wasn't for us. In this realm we feel more like Speke and Burton asking the natives which way to turn.

Granted, by the time we met, we had both traveled rather complex paths in our religious lives. While your own journeys may have fewer twists and turns, exploring your own path—how you were raised, the choices your family made for you and those that you made for yourself, the examples that were presented to you about religion and relationships—will help you understand who you are now as a person exploring an interfaith relationship. You may be surprised by what you discover.

JON Not only have I somehow missed the clearly marked path, or done a lousy job of following the obvious signs, but my religious life hasn't necessarily been a process of going forward. Nor do I claim to be climbing upward, as if I can tell that I'm getting progressively closer to God. In some ways I'm actually going backward.

I was born into a non-denominational evangelical church, moved to Episcopalianism before I was twenty, and eventually became a Roman Catholic. Today, even though I'm still a Catholic and go to mass, I pray and practice mostly with Jews, and Michal likes to repeat a remark made by a friend over dinner years ago that perhaps I'm eternally regressing, and Zoroastrianism must be next in line for me. This is really just a joke, but sometimes I wonder.

Baptist → Episcopalian → Catholic → Jewish → Zoroastrian? → Did cavemen have a religion??

I was born with an evangelical Protestant imagination and have been trying to expand it ever since. "Just as I am, without one plea, but that thy blood was shed for me"—I sang that hymn over and over as a child in church in Wheaton, Illinois, leaving my pew for the center aisle, walking forward to commit and recommit my life to Jesus Christ. If you share a background like mine, you know what I mean. Wheaton was the macrocosmic mecca of evangelicalism and a microcosmic world that included Vacation Bible School, "sword drills" (games training kids to quickly find Bible references), worship services dominated by sermonizing, mission trips from the suburbs to Central America, and one-on-one evangelizing, even revival tent meetings—I helped organize one once.

Earnest belief came early. When I was five, I kneeled with my father in the living room to ask Jesus into my heart. That's of course what we called it—what millions of people still call it. Phrase by phrase, I repeated after my dad: "Heavenly Father... I realize that I am a sinner... I ask for your forgiveness.... I want to change and become a new person.... I ask you to come into my heart." This may sound ludicrous to many of you, but believe me, I meant every word of it. Or at least I knew how to demonstrate that my meaning was sincere. With a perspective that has changed much over the last forty-odd years, I now realize that meaning is more complex, and best practiced rather than stated. But back then it was simply spoken words that were heartfelt.

I was fascinated with the crucifixion. We learned about it often in Sunday school, and I had it described to me in vivid detail from the pulpit. The passion of Christ—the stages from his arrest to his humiliation to his trial and then death—enthralled my imagination. Jesus knew every kid's nightmare: to be taken away, stripped naked, beaten up, pointed at, and laughed at. And, as I was taught, I had done these very things to him—made it necessary for Jesus to undergo such awfulness. So I experimented. I would close my bedroom door and strip my action figures naked, leaving Batman and G.I. Joe to hang on crosses of my own design, easy to link together with Lincoln Logs. Then, I would sit quietly gazing at them, praying with as deep of a sorrow as I could muster. By the time I was in Christian high school, I gave a chapel talk in which I presumed to describe, Mel Gibson–style, what it was like to be crucified.

My father worked in the world of evangelical book publishing and so I was exposed at an early age to some of the pillars of our faith. I sat at dinner with Charles Ryrie, the seminary professor and famous Bible translator, and went to lunch with what was then a young, heavyset magazine editor named Jerry Jenkins, later to become famous as the author of the Left Behind series of apocalyptic novels.

It was strange being a certified Christian in a public school full of kids who I knew were going to hell. I was supposed to witness to my playmates, to save them from the eternal torment that they were headed for, but I never did. When I was baptized in church in the fourth grade, such a momentous event was unknown to anyone at school.

After nine years of public school, I attended a religious high school. Wheaton Christian High School (now called Wheaton Academy) was a sort of prep school for nearby Wheaton College. My family would have struggled to afford the tuition had my mother not been the school principal's executive secretary, making it free. It was a rigorous education, with lots of one-on-one attention from teachers. One teacher,

Mr. Masquelier, made a sizable impact on my life, feeding my curiosity to learn, and insisting more than any teacher had ever done that I work harder. I was able to take classes that included Modern European Literature and a Shakespeare seminar. The reader in me was born. I pored over a lot of books that were outside the curriculum as well, including the complete poems of Wordsworth (as a freshman, while moodily strolling among elm trees), Wendell Berry essays (introduced to me by a local bookseller), and the dialogues of Plato. My mind was expanding just as my spirit was at its most sensitive.

Attempting to atone for the sin of failing to convert my playmates in grade school was one reason why I chose a college that surprised even my conservative parents: Moody Bible Institute. My parents had met and married at Moody, in downtown Chicago, but they never imagined that their son would choose to go there. Moody was primarily a place for training missionaries or evangelists, not lovers of the liberal arts.

Since childhood, I'd been to "Founder's Week" at Moody every February and watched with admiration great evangelical preachers from around the world. I recall being enthralled once as a famous British minister preached for an hour. Each sermon was broadcast live around the world on radio, and a series of small lights lit up on the pulpit to signal when stations would be breaking for commercials at the top of the hour. I watched as a tiny yellow light quietly lit, signaling two minutes remaining. "Let me conclude by simply saying this..." the minister began. A minute later, the orange light came on. Sixty seconds. "Let us pray..." he said. Finishing praying, all eyes reopened (but mine), and the small red light gently shone. I was impressed beyond words. Moody would school me further in the ways of God-talk, and give me an opportunity to put them into practice. Surely that, I believed at eighteen, was more important than all the books in the world.

My only year in Bible college proved to be a shocking adjustment, however. I was at heart a student full of questions and curiosity, and Moody was geared toward young people who already felt that they knew the answers to life's questions and only needed to deepen their commitments. So instead of discussing new ideas, there I was in classes such as Evangelism 101, learning how to witness on the streets of Chicago.

The summer before college, I had applied to become a missionary, and at the end of my year at Moody I was sent by the Conservative Baptist Foreign Mission Society as an assistant church planter to Batangas City, the Philippines. I was instructed to convert the native Catholics, to show them the importance of praying to ask Jesus into their hearts. We taught that the sacraments of the Catholic Church, such as taking communion, going to confession, and doing penance, would not bring either happiness or security, on earth or in heaven. We claimed that the Church made these things up, and they'd become like idols to people, something to completely eschew. We preached that each person must profess born-again faith in Jesus Christ, and be re-baptized, or baptized correctly. Catholics are usually "sprinkled" with water as infants, as we liked to differentiate, rather than "immersed" in it, as we believed the scriptures showed it should be done.

That summer was a turning point. Faced with devout Catholics living engaged Catholic lives, I simply couldn't disrupt them. The pain of some of the people, as they struggled—weighing the relative merits of eternal salvation (as we were presenting it) versus everything that they knew and loved (their families, their communities, their Church)—struck me deeply. The experience highlighted what I had begun to realize before I left: asking people about their religious beliefs can almost feel indecent. Most people find it inappropriate, if not wrong, to challenge such things. I also began to realize that what they said they believed was not that important. Most people don't have a ready answer to questions of belief. I'd been taught how that was a serious problem. But my Catholic friends in the Philippines were the first to show me that a creed doesn't make Christians. A life does.

Sitting in Filipino living rooms, I watched as Catholics prayed, and I wanted to pray as they did. In church I witnessed their liturgical celebrations and wanted the joy and mystery they seemed to experience. I began to study the lives of famous Catholics like Francis of Assisi and Teresa of Avila and saw how they seemed to be seized by a love for God and a desire to be a channel for that love in the world in practical ways, ways that had little to do with my faith.

The souls of the people I met no longer looked desperate, as I once believed of all souls that hadn't prayed the prayer of salvation. This, I now realize, was a sort of Catholic stirring inside of me, as Christian life before the 16th century was infused by the idea that there is a small piece of divinity resident inside of us. Meister Eckhart called it a spark. Julian of Norwich called it a part of our will that never really wanted to sin. It was the first Protestants who made popular the notion that there is not a shard of goodness in humankind.

I was a miserable failure as a missionary. In fact, by the time my summer was over I was convinced what I was doing was wrong—that there was something wrong with my childhood faith. I began to fall in love with Catholicism. I was sent to show them how they'd gotten it all wrong, and instead, they showed me.

Having transferred out of Bible college, my evangelical vision was being gradually replaced by something much broader. I wandered from church to church looking for others like me. Mennonites counseled me on how to register as a Conscientious Objector with Selective Service. Swedish pietists at the Evangelical Covenant Church showed me that it was possible to have differing points of view on religious matters and still gather together and worship. And the monasticism of Thomas Merton's writings drew me more than once to visit his old monastery in Kentucky.

Becoming a Catholic would have absolutely killed my parents, not to mention my grandparents, so it never seemed an option. Then, while waiting tables at a Mexican restaurant at night, and working part-time at a campus bookstore, I began attending North Park Theological Seminary in Chicago. I thought for a while that I might become an Episcopal priest. I remember fondly Don Dayton's Karl Barth seminar, and David Scholer's introduction to the Gospels; I took every January term class offered by Paul Holmer, who'd recently retired from Yale and come to North Park to teach Wittgenstein, Kierkegaard, and Lewis. But after two and a half years I left, realizing that I was in no shape to pastor anyone. This was just at the time when the market for religious and spiritual books was burgeoning and my love for books and ideas sent me in that direction. That was 1991, and for more than two decades now, I've worked with books in one way or another.

Most of that time I was a good Episcopalian, for almost twenty years, preaching in church on occasion, and serving on diocesan discernment committees. But I've had the opportunity to keep my fingers and toes in many spiritual pots. I've never been a one-church person, and I've never really been a one-tradition person, either.

It was for that reason that when I was curious to find a new and more challenging job in 1997, I replied to the founder of a Jewish spirituality publisher in Vermont, curious to see what he sought in a head of marketing. It turned out that he wanted someone who understood the Christian market, yet also had a broader perspective. Friends told me that taking the job was nuts; what did I really know about Judaism? My parents told me that taking it would appear to compromise my Christian belief; can you be a Christian and market books reflecting another religious tradition? But I accepted the position and became the vice president of marketing for Jewish Lights Publishing.

Two years later I cofounded a new publishing imprint dedicated to multi-faith explorations of spiritual and religious topics. We named it SkyLight Paths Publishing and it became rapidly successful. I acquired, created, edited, and marketed books by people of faith and spiritual practice talking with each other across the traditions. We created new editions of classic spiritual texts, most of which have names that sound forbidding, such as Zohar, Philokalia, Ramakrishna, Ecclesiastes, and Gita, but we tried to make them more accessible.

Then we did the same for spiritual practices, showing how the same practice tends to pop up in different forms in many different religious traditions. There were reasons why people began calling our small company in Vermont "the Ben & Jerry's of religious publishing."

Along the way I began writing myself. *Praying with Our Hands* introduced twenty-one ways that people across religious traditions use their hands, not just their thoughts or spoken words, to pray. Working on that project rekindled my interest in Catholicism, making me want to explore and write about Catholic subjects, and as I did, I was drawn to live a more Catholic life. I began carrying a rosary in my pocket, praying it only when I was alone. At work I would sometimes pause at midday to pray the noontime liturgical hour—in the men's room. I even went to confession for the first time while on a business trip in London where no one would know me. For a decade I was a Protestant writer who appreciated Catholic tradition. I would give talks at conferences and in parishes and say, "I like how you think, how you look at the world, and I want more of that in my own life." And I meant it.

Catholic friends would ask me why I didn't simply join the Catholic Church, and I always had a reason. The authority of the pope bothered me. Then I studied the meaning of the magisterium and realized that the Church is much bigger than the pope, and thank God for that. The more I engaged in Catholic life, the more I recognized things that bothered me. Not ordaining women, for instance, and a whole range of issues relating to sex, family, divorce, who is in and who is out, concerned me, until I realized again that there are millions of Catholics who disagree with Rome on these issues, and even the catechism. I would be in good company. Then there was the issue of my family and what they might think. I had long given up on being able to please my parents spiritually and religiously. Then my marriage ended in 2007 and I had no more excuses. My two wonderful teenagers, Clelia and Joseph, were supportive, ready for whatever turn my religious life might take. So when a Catholic friend asked me again why I didn't simply join the Church, I replied, "I don't know."

But there was *still* a problem. I didn't know how to reconcile my respect for, and involvement in, other religious traditions with the whole idea of conversion. Conversion can be an important way of defining who you are. For some, it is a way of saying *This is the side that I am on*. But to convert, in most traditions, usually involves more than self-identification; it also involves a form of repudiating the past. It is a turning away as much as it is a turning toward, and for me, religious identity is too complicated for conversion to be a satisfying—or accurate—answer to the question of who I am.

I am still uncomfortable with conversion, but nevertheless decided to become a Catholic because I wanted to correct an accident of history. The accident was that my Irish and Italian great-grandfathers came to this country, steeped in Catholic culture and tradition, and their children became evangelical Christians. Why? I suspect that living far from centers of Catholic immigrant life in the American heartland, they wanted to be accepted.

As for me, I felt more accepted, more at home, in historic Catholicism. I realized that not only was it the lens I had been looking through as I scrutinized the world, but it was the primary lens that I wanted to use to understand my place. So I became a Catholic on October 4, 2009, the feast day of St. Francis of Assisi. Several good people were there to support me, including one of my best friends, a gay man who knew beforehand how unwelcome he would feel in those pews. I will admit that I shuddered as I repeated some of what my parish priest had me repeat after him, but I said it nonetheless, glad it was over when it was.

Michal wasn't there that day. She was in Chicago at a family reunion. We became engaged just five days before that memorable ceremony, which means that, as I stood there, I knew in my heart that I would probably always be, in the eyes of the Church, a bad Catholic.

MICHAL Signs? I didn't even realize I was on a path until well into my adult life. My religious upbringing begins almost as a caricature, a Jewish girl living in Skokie, Illinois. And, no, despite the rumors floating around since the late 1970s, the Nazis never actually marched there.

My grandparents immigrated from Russia and Poland and brought strong accents and traditional food but little by way of religion. My mother has memories of festive holiday meals with her extended family and her confirmation at a local Conservative synagogue. My father had no experience with Judaism at home and spent most of his childhood in boarding schools simply aware that he was a Jew.

My parents moved from the north side of Chicago when my older sister was two and joined an urban Reform synagogue just after their fourth daughter was born, seeking a Sunday-only program like the one Mom had attended—just what they felt was needed for their little harem. While my parents chose the synagogue because of its school, what made it unique was the music program, which quickly became the foundation of my experience there. In fourth grade the Sunday program shifted to Shabbat morning; classroom time was followed by a prayer service, held in a glorious, old sanctuary with red velvet seats and a balcony. Each week I donned a steel blue robe and sang with the junior choir in the choir loft, accompanied by the grand organ.

Before that year was out, I told my parents I wanted to go to Hebrew school, a separate weekday afternoon program, and prepare for a bat mitzvah, which was never their vision for their girls. Yet that summer I went to Jewish overnight camp and received private tutoring in Hebrew, joining my cohort that fall and sharing the *bima* with a close friend on a Friday evening for a joint bat mitzvah service two years later.

It was many years before I discovered how fortunate I was that my parents joined this *heimish shul* (Yiddish for unpretentious synagogue) in the city instead of a typical, more palatial-style, suburban synagogue. This was due not only to the warmth and socioeconomic diversity of the membership and the Shabbat school, which created a much more meaningful experience, but also because Judy Karzen, the choir director, brought spirit, passion, and intensity that wasn't the norm in Reform synagogues and was a sharp contrast to the typically intellectual, male, politically oriented rabbi, with whom I did not relate. Music was the hook that would keep me tethered to Judaism.

Meanwhile, at home we would have Shabbat dinner each week, complete with candles, wine, and challah, which my father would throw across the table, not knowing it was an old Chasidic tradition. Dinner was followed by family night, with home movies, games, or perhaps recording a tape to send to our cousins in Tennessee.

In high school I dated an Orthodox boy, Arthur, whom I met through theater, and had my first personal experience of Jewish diversity. The arena where this became clear was food. As a Reform Jew we had little connection to *kashrut*, the system of limiting, separating, and preparing food according to the biblical laws. We grew up eating shrimp cocktail, ham, and cheeseburgers. But we took Passover more seriously, replacing our bread with *matzah*, never mind that we didn't understand that raisin bran and spaghetti were equally forbidden. So for a week I would sit at the cafeteria table with my PB&J on *matzah*. To my right was my bat mitzvah partner, whose own *matzah* was filled with her usual ham and cheese! To my left was my Orthodox boyfriend, who brought his own apple juice to drink because the juice boxes at school were not marked "kosher for Passover." I didn't understand how the preparation of apple juice could relate to running to freedom through the Red Sea carrying unleavened cakes that weren't allowed to rise prior to baking.

College, of course, is generally a time of exploration and discovery. On the religious front I learned that I was comfortable with my Reform Jewish identity and *not* interested in social Judaism. Generally, Jewish life on campus is based out of the Hillel house, and like many such houses, the Northwestern University Hillel was a more conservative environment than was comfortable for me. I spent most Jewish holidays back at home with my family. If uninterested in the religious life at the Hillel, I was equally indifferent to the Jewish and non-Jewish houses in the Greek sorority system and ignored the Jewish fraternities, preferring to hang out at a low-key, quirky, diverse house where a number of my friends from marching band were members.

I also discovered I was intrigued by religiously engaged non-Jews. Early on in my freshman year I met two young men from the dorm next door in the cafeteria line and we became fast friends. Tom and Jeff were involved with the InterVarsity Christian Fellowship chapter on campus. Somehow, I was able to engage with their religious lives and beliefs, different as they were, more so than I could with most of the Jews around me. I can still see the white screen with the projection of a prayer, glimpsed through my dorm lounge window during an InterVarsity gathering, with words I recognized—"Who is like you, Lord?" I felt connected. Yet when Tom and Jeff regularly complained about their struggles with the chemistry that I found so easy, I would tease them, suggesting studying might have been more effective than praying prior to their exams.

During my final year at Northwestern I rented the third floor of the Episcopalian house on campus, sharing a small apartment with my friend Jamie. I actually shared it with her and her boyfriend, George, whom I had known for years from the band. He, in particular, was keen to educate me about their religious lives; it took many years for me to read the Christian Bible, fulfilling an obligation to George, who went directly from NU to seminary to become an Episcopal priest.

I was at his ordination but we eventually lost touch. Yet I feel that the roots of my own clerical life are entangled with his. And my ultimate Jewish home in the Reconstructionist movement mirrors his Episcopal sensibility in many ways, primarily in the embrace of both traditional ritual and progressive social values.

In 1985, during my summer between college and grad school, I traveled to Israel and worked as a volunteer on a kibbutz and traveled throughout the land. I engaged deeply with the ancient history and was mostly oblivious to the politics. I have no recollection of what prompted me to spend my last real summer vacation and all of my bat mitzvah gift funds on this trip. That was the second mysterious decision that baffled my parents and led me toward a more committed Jewish life.

I went to graduate school at MIT and at some point during my tenure there discovered "Torah and Chocolate." On Friday at noon, we—meaning me plus a bunch of undergraduate males with a lot of dark facial hair, all of whom sounded like they were from Long Island—brought our bagged lunches to a conference room, where we would crowd around a table with two piles: one of *chumashim*, which contained the Torah text and commentaries, and the other of huge bars of gourmet (and kosher) chocolates. I have no idea what prompted me to go; my graduate school years were difficult and these hours may have been a source of solace, distraction, or connection.

Returning to Chicago for my first job, I became involved with a Jewish singles group. Many of the members also formed the core of a young adult program at an urban Conservative *shul*. There I discovered liturgy, much of which had been edited out of the Reform prayer book. I began to participate regularly but was never comfortable with the gestalt of the group. The practice felt mechanical, including my own learning and mastery of the *siddur* (prayer book). While I learned *what* to do, there was little discussion about *why* it was done, and the environment was largely joyless.

After two years in Chicago I moved again, this time for a job with the makers of Gore-Tex fabric. High on a plateau, adjacent to both the Hopi and Navajo reservations, in Flagstaff I was exposed to earth-based and Eastern religion, women's spirituality, and macrobiotics. And I discovered how Jewish life is different in a place with very few Jews. I became active in the small synagogue, which met in a converted house a couple of times a month and for major holidays. Members came from miles in every direction and from widely disparate Jewish backgrounds, happy to connect with others of "the tribe."

During my tenure with Gore I spent a year as an internal consultant at their Newark, Delaware, corporate headquarters. My first visit to Beth El, the only *shul* in town, happened to occur during their annual "Creative Arts Shabbat" program. I arrived a bit late, entering the sanctuary to find a woman on the *bima* wearing a leotard and flowing skirts. This was an interpretive dance of the *Barchu*, the communal call to prayer. There I had the "coming home" experience that many do at their first Reconstructionist *shul*: one of fitting in, engaging with a practice that is meaningful and relevant, and enjoying being with others who are deeply involved and committed, all within a liberal framework. I didn't know I was looking for something new until I found it.

The rabbi at Beth El had a broad and interesting array of Jewish connections. A graduate of the Reform seminary, he was also involved in the decades-old National Havurah Committee, as well as the fairly newly flourishing Jewish Renewal movement. Toward the end of my year in Delaware, he handed me a brochure for the 1995 Jewish Renewal Kallah, a large biennial gathering to be held on a college campus in Colorado. I was intrigued and went, taking dance and meditation classes, joining guided, meditative hikes, indulging in bountiful vegetarian buffets—not your typical Jewish fare. If I had missed the sixties as a child, this was my chance to experience the flow, the color, and the intensity I have always imagined, based solely on my multiple viewings of the musical *Hair*.

Each morning Reb Zalman Schachter-Shalomi, the primary founder of the Renewal movement, would give a *shiur clali*, a lesson for everyone, while sitting on an overstuffed orange chair in the middle of an empty stage in an auditorium filled with nearly nine hundred *hasidim*, devoted students. One morning I listened intently as Reb Zalman explained: "The world is an economic mess because money doesn't rest on *Shabbos* anymore." Traditional Jewish practice could affect the world! Who knew? This became a window into a world of traditional practice that had never interested me previously.

That fall I returned to Flagstaff to begin physical therapy school and had yet another life-changing experience. Late one Saturday night, a score of folks sat around a bonfire singing the *selichot*, the penitential prayers that form the core of the High Holy Day liturgy. As the formal service came to an end and many of us remained to continue singing and to share some hot chocolate, a member turned to the rabbi:

"Billy, perhaps Michal can be the cantor (the liturgical music leader) for *yuntif* (the holy days)."

"Well I certainly can't sing. Michal, what do you think? We have, what, almost a week?" Of course I had been singing this liturgy for decades, and still had most of it in sheet music form as well. I happily agreed.

During the first evening of Rosh Hashanah service I found myself profoundly moved, at times to the point of tears. This was not at all a typical experience for me, and I was as surprised as the rest of the congregation by my expression of emotion. After the service I was approached numerous times by members inquiring as to whether I was on the wrong professional path. Perhaps I had a future of spiritual leadership ahead of me? I stayed the course, completing the physical therapy program, but my Jewish life had transformed.

Because our synagogue did not meet weekly, I created my own Shabbat experience, which included yoga, Torah study, and long afternoons outside, often singing *Shabbos* songs while hiking or cross-country skiing. Occasionally I had Shabbat dinner with a local family or studied Torah with a friend, but much of this experience was solitary. When there was a service at the synagogue, I was often leading, bringing to the community the ideas and practices that I had absorbed during the year at Beth El and week at the retreat.

During the third year of the physical therapy program, I traversed the country, completing a series of clinical residencies. In each city, I engaged in Jewish learning as, or perhaps more, deeply as I did my clinical assignments. I learned to chant the Torah and the prophetic texts and to lead a traditional service. I refreshed my knowledge of Hebrew, which had been latent since high school. Within a year of completing my degree I moved to a Jewish retreat center and then to

Philadelphia, home of both Reconstructionist and Renewal Judaism.

In Philadelphia I had a rich Jewish life, surrounded by community with whom I shared Shabbat dinners and holidays, living in a neighborhood with multiple progressive synagogues. I recall numerous conversations with my parents that went something like this: "Sorry I missed your call, I was at *shul*."

"Oh. Why this morning?"

"Well, it's Shabbat."

"But is it a holiday? A bar mitzvah?"

"No, just Shabbat."

"Are you Orthodox?" It was easier for them to comprehend my active Jewish life after I actually became a rabbi.

At thirty-eight, I was far from the oldest student at seminary, but easily a decade older than the median. The highlight of my years there may well be leading a community-wide "movement *davenning*," a facilitated prayer experience somewhat reminiscent of what I encountered that first Shabbat in Delaware. Sharing this experience with not only students but with professors and the president of the college, not necessarily folks you would imagine twirling under their prayer shawls, grounded me in my understanding and joy of leading liturgy and ritual.

I never lost my love of small-town life and upon graduation sought out a pulpit in rural New England, taking a part-time post in Vermont. Unfortunately, the position was not a good fit and I left after two years. Remaining in the town, I worked as a physical therapist for a homecare agency—a position I had taken during my rabbinic tenure—and served monthly as visiting clergy for a *shul* an hour north. But without the rabbinic role I confronted the same problem I had in Flagstaff and became frustrated by a lack of Jewish connection; there were few others living a Jewish life beyond the limited synagogue schedule. I did find inspiration and companionship with two groups of Christian colleagues, a weekly support group of regional female clergy and a monthly lunch with three local, liberal ministers. But it was only a matter of time before I would move on.

I couldn't discuss my spiritual life and development without mentioning yoga, which I've practiced since 1988. I don't recall what inspired me to go to my first class, offered through the local high school adult education program, but that first experience was deep and rich. I remember the gentle yet strong nature of the teacher and the long, luscious *shavasanah* (corpse pose) while snuggled in thick socks, under blankets, at the end of class. This was before power yoga, before health club yoga—this yoga was an esoteric, ancient teaching being shared with a handful of seekers, of which I was the youngest by decades.

Throughout my life, yoga has been a window into my heart and mind. It both quiets and occupies my body so that I'm able to notice what is happening inside: whether I am steady or ragged, focused or scattered, strong or ailing. And the experience of bringing the spirituality into the postures is mirrored in my Jewish practice, where I tend to be quite animated in bringing my body into my prayer.

My exposure to traditional Judaism, Reconstructionist thought, Eastern and Jewish mystical traditions, meditation, and yoga have nurtured a somewhat unconventional rabbi. My rabbinate is centered in the personal and close communal, in prayer and ritual. I love to teach basics, in hopes of bringing connection and meaning to those for whom Judaism seems foreign, irrelevant, or inaccessible. And my rabbinic life took a turn my childhood rabbi could never have fathomed. Jon entered my life as I left my first pulpit.

When we ponder our own stories and look back to consider our individual paths, we are surprised at how different the starting points were, and yet how similar the end points are, despite the religious differences. It reminds us of an old story—a folktale—of two sojourners who meet deep in a thick forest. Both have been wandering alone for days and somewhat confused as to the path. They are each thrilled to suddenly and fortuitously have found another person, hoping that they can point them in the right direction. And as neither of them knows the way out any longer, they look for the way together.

CHAPTER 2

Seeking Love, Keeping Faith

When it comes to love, our relational lives seem to mirror our religious lives. One often follows the other—consciously or not. For example, those who come from a background with little or no religious formation tend to enter relationships later than those who are deeply imbedded in a religious community, belief system, and practice that makes marriage and children a religious priority.

For the latter, serious commitment in a relationship frequently comes at an earlier age (even before the age of twenty), after fewer, and likely less diverse, romantic experiences. Those who grow up deeply involved in a faith tradition are more likely to come to romantic relationships with detailed religious expectations. Many religious traditions, in fact, encourage precisely this. One thinks immediately of evangelical Christianity, Orthodox Judaism, traditional Islam, and, well, just about every religion's more conservative branch of expression. Family and religious community are also likely to be actively involved in the process and outcome of dating and marrying, and the relationship continues to live within religious community.

On the flip side of this are those who come to romantic relationships from environments with little religious expectation regarding marriage. For them, decisions about who and how to date or when and whether to marry are more likely to be made as independent adults, after sorting through these issues on their own.

Our stories unfolded along these lines. Jon, for example, married at the young age of twenty-one, straight out of Christian college. That's what was expected of him, having grown up in a well-defined evangelical milieu. He was married for seventeen years, and he and his ex-wife raised two children. Michal, meanwhile, came to the institution of marriage later in life, having had other serious relationships and a previous engagement. Judaism was important throughout her formative years, but any cultural expectations of marriage and children were matched by expectations of acquiring education and achieving professional success. She eventually married at thirty-five but divorced quickly, without kids.

Despite these differences, one thing we both learned quickly is that just because a relationship looks good on paper doesn't mean it is a match. When recalling her broken engagement from many years ago, Michal often remembers that their résumés were more compatible than their hearts or souls ever were. As for us, before we met, we were both looking back on the cultural and personal pressures that may have led us to make previous choices—wanting to do it better the next time. We were both turning to our futures somewhat hesitant about the next commitment. We suspect that these issues are quite common in the world of relationships, whether one is religious or not, inter-dating or not.

Religious issues that might raise a quick, red relationship flag include getting to know someone who seems to not respect your religious convictions or background. This can express itself in a variety of subtle ways, such as teasing about going to church or following dietary laws, having your religious beliefs referred to as "superstitions," or perhaps simply by showing a clear lack of interest when religious topics—important to you—come up. Another source of concern would be if you find yourself concealing your religious ideas or practices or actually repressing them in order to attract or please a potential partner. How important is your religious life to you? Is it something you would consider abandoning for a relationship?

Before turning a friendship into something more, regardless of whether you share a religious identity or commitment, ask yourself, is this potential partner interested in knowing who you really are? Be sure to discover or uncover whether you have the ability or desire to openly share and explore your religious interests with that other person, and vice versa. Such a simple place as this would be the first spot to assess your compatibility, and to gauge whether you have the potential to create a deeper understanding of each other.

MICHAL We were standing in my parents' bedroom, admiring the new vertical blinds. Within ten minutes of being back at home for summer break, I was already planning my trip to Ohio, where my first college boyfriend lived.

"Do you think you would ever marry someone non-Jewish?" asked my mother.

I paused. "Only if I loved him."

I don't think this was the answer my mom was expecting from me, her one actively Jewish daughter. But I don't recall having given the issue a lot of thought. Nor do I believe I discussed religion with this young man or with my previous boyfriend, also not Jewish, who I unceremoniously dumped simply because I was going to college and he, a year younger, wasn't.

As a college junior I briefly dated Brian Katz, who was Jewish, and from Puerto Rico. Somehow that last detail meant something to my mother. And she was correct—this Jew from Puerto Rico *was* from a wealthy family. I know that the attitudes and values that came along with that wealth were among the things that did *not* work for me in that relationship.

Then I met Ron. I was a senior. He was a grad student—tall, thin as a rail, blond, gawky, goofy, with Southern roots. He was undoubtedly my first real love. We *did* have the conversation, a number of times. I went to church with him and his family. He joined me for High Holiday services. My clearest memory of our interaction around religious differences is of him leaving my attic apartment one evening, muttering the words, "Someday I will ask you to marry me and you are going to have to figure out an answer!" Turning quickly, he then smacked his forehead on the door frame.

Though our relationship survived a year apart, me at MIT and he finishing his MS, we split prior to my completing the two-year program; I suspect religion was only one among other issues we faced in our relationship.

From there on my pattern seemed to be one significant relationship every five years or so, with long droughts in between. The ongoing tale, which started in high school, is of my being "intimidating"—too smart, or too alternative, or too Jewish, and then, eventually, a rabbi—yes, that title's a real boy magnet.

In the early 1990s I was set up on a blind date with the brother of a young woman I knew through work. Daniel was a physician, lived in a big city, and yes, was a nice Jewish boy. We shared Reform Jewish backgrounds, read the *Wall Street Journal*, listened to NPR. I was almost thirty, had been dedicated to school and work for years without any real romantic possibilities, and believed that this was the type of person and relationship I *should* be involved in.

On a weekend visit to his hometown I joined his mother for Torah study, sharing an insight with more passion than I realized I felt, that God's decision to ban Moses from the land was more complicated than the text, or the later rabbinic commentary, claimed. Daniel was out buying me a diamond while his mother and I were at *shul* that Shabbat morning.

In the end, we were two people with similar backgrounds, on different paths. Mine was turning toward the progressive, alternative, natural, spiritual. Daniel was on a pretty conventional road toward an MBA to complement his MD and seemed happy to re-create his own suburban upbringing for himself. We became engaged and tried to make it work, but called it off just as the wedding invitations were about to be printed.

So five years later when I sat down next to a young man at a progressive *shul* in a hippie town in Oregon, the odds of sharing more than Jewish ethnicity were high. Turns out that going to synagogue was a renewed experience following a decades-long hiatus during which his spiritual practice took place primarily in a zendo. He was a vegetarian, a co-op member, a lover of fine tea and simple living. Could I have found my soul mate at last?

The question is rhetorical. Shared religious and spiritual passions drove our lives together. We moved cross-country to join the staff at a Jewish retreat center. Then we moved again, and again. There were red flags even before we married, but I chose to ignore them. I approached the marriage with serious doubts as well as measures of both desperation (I was well into my mid-thirties) and absolute spiritual conviction that I was meant to be with this man. Ultimately I decided to accept the high risk, which I hoped might provide great reward. It didn't.

Having been married and divorced changed me. The Torah teaches that a woman has agency over her own life only after being married and then either widowed or divorced. Otherwise, she's subject to the will of her father or spouse. So according to biblical tradition, I had finally earned the independence that had been a hallmark of my life. I vowed that I would not be the one to drive a relationship again.

I entered rabbinical school soon thereafter. The major paper from my first year focused on that very issue I had explored with Daniel's mother nine years earlier—God's decision to ban Moses from the land. And I had a recurring conversation, one that somehow often occurred in the library...

"Michal, I don't understand why you are single. You are so smart and lovely and [insert a superlative here]."

"Do you know someone I should meet?"

Long silence.

"No." Then I would usually just smile and shrug.

So when I decided to take a job in Vermont, people were worried. "How will you meet anyone *there*?!" they asked. I had spent years in Chicago and Philadelphia, even created an online dating profile for myself as a New Yorker during the year of my student pulpit in northern New Jersey. At this point, I was interested in living the life I wanted, back in the woods. I bought a home on my own for the second time, ready to settle into my new role as a rabbi.

I purchased an 1860s duplex, definitely a fixer-upper. It hadn't seen a coat of paint, let alone a screwdriver, in at least fifty years—the proverbial worst house on the best block. It had a few issues that needed to be remedied before the moving truck arrived, and that I couldn't address myself without some tools and assistance. How convenient that a contractor was working right next door. I stopped by and introduced myself, asked about the project—a new dining room—and explained that I was looking for a bit of help.

Bob never let me pay for that first job and ended up accompanying me through a difficult first year in town. He was warm, generous, and thoughtful. Divorced, he had two teenagers and was a member of the local Mennonite church, which seemed to share the peoplehood or cultural aspect of Judaism and Catholicism. The few folks at my synagogue who were aware of our developing relationship were unfazed, but then again most of them were intermarried.

We never seriously imagined marrying, although we did occasionally ponder what that might entail, and eventually we broke up. But the loss was hard for me. Bob had filled a huge emotional hole for me from the moment I arrived in Vermont.

So as I began my second, equally tenuous year at the local *shul*, I was ever more curious to see what this life as a single, rural rabbi would hold in store.

JON In the evangelical Christian home of my childhood, the teaching on who to date was crystal clear: only born-again Christians. Why? Because dating was for no other purpose than to find a marriage partner. You'd better only date girls you can marry, I was told. This meant dating only girls from church, or, in my private Christian high school, only those who were most earnest about their faith.

So I never had casual girlfriends. To treat dating casually seemed like a sin—as if I would be dating just for fun. I had two girlfriends in high school, relationships that each lasted for more than a year, and talked seriously about marriage with each. In one case, as a high school freshman all of four-teen, I even recall conversations with her parents on the topic of whether and when their daughter and I might wed. I don't recall ever discussing religious questions or doubts in either relationship—I was too young to have them. In both, we went to church and worshipped sitting side by side. In both, we were saved, and in the same sort of way, which was enough to mean that religiously and spiritually we were simpatico.

What else was there to talk about? By the end of high school, I felt as if I'd experienced two serious breakups—because the relationships had been treated so seriously.

The second cardinal rule of Christian dating was this: sexual intimacy is reserved only for marriage. What *sort* of intimacy was *too* sexual was never very clearly defined, and so we often explored that matter for ourselves. Don't allow yourself to be alone with a girl, I was told. Well, I broke that rule, and others to be sure, and so before my teenage years were over I knew guilt as well as the next guy. If one needed further religious reasons to avoid casual dating, this was it: the desire for sex was a prime mover toward early marriage.

The expectations of men's and women's roles in a marriage also troubled me. Even in those first high school relationships I was drawn to girls that were strong and smart, rather than demure and simple. But the Bible told me that marriage is a place for men to be strong and women to be submissive. That was pretty unappealing. So by college, when I was questioning everything about my childhood faith, I abandoned dating for a while. Religion and love were messed up in my mind. So I divorced them.

I dated only two women in college, and religion played no part in either relationship. Philosophy played a part in the first—since Susan and I met in Arthur Holmes's yearlong History of Philosophy class. We shared a knack for debating oblique ideas. We discussed films, epistemology, novels, Hegel, music, and brains in vats, but never faith. As the old categories of belief splintered away from me, I no longer had words for who I was, spiritually and religiously. I had become a pilgrim and it didn't feel right to talk too much about it. As for Susan, she probably didn't want to talk about faith with me, either, recovering fundamentalist that she also was.

My second college relationship turned into my first marriage. The little sister of my best friend, Danelle and I began dating almost by accident. Mutual friends sort of pushed us together. Her parents had met and married at Wheaton College, just as mine had done at Moody Bible Institute. You might say that evangelicalism ran in the family, and no one questioned why the two of us with so little else in common would engage and marry so quickly. She was going to follow me—which wasn't something I really wanted. I'm not sure if I really loved her, but when that question entered my mind, I quickly concluded that God brought us together and God must know what he's doing. Despite my doubts, the old categories of faith were guiding me.

We married just weeks after graduating from Wheaton in June 1989. I recall two marriage preparation classes with the Presbyterian minister who married us, but I can't remember what we talked about. In the weeks before and after our wedding I dreamed about the monastic life that I had been exploring in Kentucky during college, already with a nostalgia for what I was losing by turning toward what was expected of me: marriage and responsibility. I was convinced by then that I'd go to seminary and become a pastor. And every serious pastor has a wife.

So together we sat in church, year after year, but our sharing of religious life meant little when it came to sharing a spiritual one. My missionary experience, interest in Catholicism, and work in multi-faith publishing sent my spirit and imagination in many directions. I was both passionately religious and spiritual, but always away from home. Danelle may also have had a rich spiritual life, but we never discussed it. I don't remember it ever coming up.

Almost from the start, we were not happy and I reverted to my evangelical categories of understanding, and projecting onto the divine will, in order to process it all. Personal happiness is unimportant, I told myself. Being a disciple of Christ does not mean pursuing happiness for oneself. And then I read books that supported this view, written by Christian marriage experts. They argued that going through life seeking happiness is a sure sign of sin; it is the "way of the world," when what God really wants of us is to do what's right. And there was no question that doing what's right in marriage meant living up to your commitments. Taking your vows seriously. And finding the way—however you can—to grow together rather than apart.

The advice of course never really worked. It only made me sullen, retreating more and more into my work, focusing on my responsibilities as a father to our two beautiful children, and seeking love and recognition elsewhere. Friends and colleagues would often ask me how I seemed to get so much done, what with having a challenging full-time publishing job, raising two kids, and writing books of my own on the side. I would explain that it is easy to get a lot done when you are in an unhappy marriage; I spent a lot of time alone.

We separated for a few days in early 2005, then permanently two years later. Both times, I was steadfast against divorcing, regardless of how I really felt. It was a sin, and my two children needed the marriage to survive, regardless of whether it was good for any of the four of us. One afternoon,

I remember meeting with our Episcopal priest and screaming, "Why doesn't someone tell her that this is wrong?!"

Divorce was devastating to me at first. Then it was liberating. It was—dare I say—by the time I worked through it, a kind of salvation. Despite being fully conscious of my own faults and blame, I was set free from a paradigm of understanding God, love, relationships, and happiness that was unhealthy, to say the least. By the time the divorce was final in 2009, I celebrated by taking a trip to Italy with a good friend. Upon return, another marriage was the last thing on my mind.

Did religion unite us with our partners in ways that were meaningful and lasting? Yes and no. Shared religious tradition was at the core of both of our first marriages as was shared religious activity. Yet our religious aspirations and spiritual desires did not track in our relationships very clearly or positively once we were married. We both found that, within marriage, a shared religious background didn't necessarily provide the bonds we sought in the most intimate of relationships. Nor did it compensate for other challenges. What these previous relationships did do for us moving forward was provide clarity and patience, and yes...some baggage.

These are aspects of our backgrounds that are essential to speak about before coupling up. Serious commitment demands that we examine our own lives, and that we reveal ourselves fully to our future partners. As people of faith, this means exposing our religious and spiritual selves to each other.

CHAPTER 3

Who Am I?

One aspect of 21st-century life that makes talking about faith difficult is that it has become popular for people to speak of religion as if it is bifurcated—with an "external" reality versus an "inner" one. The external is institutional faith or organized religion while the inner is "the spiritual quest...an interior journey...and an exploration of the heart," according to bestselling author Karen Armstrong. How appealing the latter seems, and how unappealing, the former!

We hear this often, but we frankly disagree. This seems like a false dichotomy, and it feeds the notion that personal belief or experience is what is essential, whereas ritual, tradition, text, and community are somehow artificial. Religion is not necessarily more "external" than spirituality is; either can be interior, personal, and a matter of the heart (or correspondingly exterior, impersonal, and an exercise mostly of the brain), depending on one's interest and involvement. Also, there are times in life when religion feels far more essential than "inner spirituality" does.

For example, isn't it interesting how important religion becomes when a loved one dies or we face end-of-life issues ourselves, when one is about to marry or have a child? This is surely because religion remains relevant in many lives even today, often and especially at those times when we seek to create, or rediscover, connections between ourselves and our families, our history, God, and the traditions that help to define us.

Karen Armstrong goes on to express another common complaint about religious life with language suited for our "spiritual not religious" age:

> Very often, priests, rabbis, imams and shamans are just as consumed by worldly ambition as regular politicians. But all this is generally seen as an abuse of a sacred ideal. These power struggles are not what religion is really about, but an unworthy distraction from the life of the spirit.[4]

We acknowledge that the world of religion has produced scandal and abuse, as just about every field of work involving interpersonal relationships has, including medicine, education, sports, even scouting. But it still feels like an excuse for throwing a wealth of tradition out with the holy water. Yes, religion has problems, but religious traditions, texts, and practices are among the richest sources of spiritual food available. And community that is distinctively religious is what people who are interested in spirituality often seem to be seeking when they turn to religion at life cycle moments.

Still, religion is being forced to change, and for the better. And as it changes, many of us have found more space to breathe and to be. There's been mounting pressure put on traditional, organized religion over the last generation (or two, or three) and we see its fruits in everything from increased lay leadership to house churches, web faith, pub theology, and independent *minyanim* (Jewish prayer communities). Some of the pressure has come from the outside, through the scrutinizing and critiques of new atheists like Richard Dawkins and the late Christopher Hitchens. They have caused every person who thinks about religion, including those of us on the "inside," to focus more intently on what matters. Fresh expressions of faith now abound. Individuals are creating ways of practicing and expressing their faith in connection with others away from traditional institutions. In many cases, these groups form around other affinities of demographics, purpose, or values.

A paradigm shift is going on in nearly every religious tradition. Progressive Mormons are challenging Salt Lake City just as progressive Catholics, including the recently famous renegade American nuns, are taking bold steps away from Rome. Committed to their faith tradition and the spiritual and communal benefits they provide, they also wish to disconnect their religious practice from the conservative social values espoused by their institutions, and to fully include their gay, female, divorced, and alternative-minded compatriots into their religious community. Progressive Muslims are paving new ground (rediscovering Islam's medieval roots) of openness to other faiths, traditions, and egalitarian practices. Across faiths and denominations, religion looks different than it did for our parents.

The most fundamental switch of all, going on across many religions and denominations, is a valuing of belonging over belief. Some traditions—Judaism and Buddhism, for example—have never placed a high value on belief, or assent to certain "truths," and for some Jews, Judaism is a cultural identity much more than a religion at all. But Christians of all backgrounds are now seeing the wisdom of prioritizing community above belief, in the hierarchy of what is most fundamental about faith. To participate, speak up, and join is now primary, whereas what you believe is secondary, at best. They are seriously questioning the ability of belief to define who we are.

JON When Passover comes around, I sometimes remark to friends that I must be the only Christian in the world who participates in three or four seders a year. Even active Jews don't usually attend so many. Why would they, after all, unless they're working, as my wife often is—leading them— and I am usually sitting beside her. This particular seder was a turning point for my self-understanding as someone in an interfaith marriage.

We were sitting around the table with friends. Michal was leading the seder, and I was participating while also trying to keep the baby happy. Around the table were people that we knew well, and others we'd just met. Michal and I were fresh off a painful experience in Florida where she hadn't gotten a pulpit job because of me, because her husband was a Catholic. For perhaps the first time in my life, I'd felt abused as a member of a minority group (in a living room filled with twenty board members of the *shul*), because although they were kind, it seemed that all they saw was a cross on my forehead.

It is common at a seder for participants to ask questions; four are in the formal liturgy. Jews are great at asking questions, and the seder is an occasion and setting when questions big and small are encouraged. Just as we were all seated, getting ready to begin, one of the men around the table said to the rest of us: "I have a question. I notice that we are all interfaith couples around this table, that we are all Jewish-Christian."

Hmmm. Everyone took another look around at their neighbors, and we realized that he'd hit on something.

"So, I'm wondering," he resumed, "you Christians who are here, why are you?" he awkwardly said. "I mean...I'm Jewish and I know why I'm here; I know what I get out of these things; but what do you get out of this?...What brings *you* here?"

And with that, we went around the table answering his question.

The first person to speak was a middle-aged woman sitting to my left, who is married to another woman. She gave the perfect progressive, mainline Protestant answer: "As you may know, this week is also Holy Week in the Christian world, and I was just at the Maundy Thursday service at my church last night. It was beautiful. We talked about the life and Judaism of Jesus, and the focus of the service was to remember the seder that Jesus and the disciples shared together on the night before he was crucified. So, I am fresh off that powerful experience and I'm delighted to be able to continue thinking on those things by being here with you, tonight!" She beamed, and everyone nodded or thanked her.

The next answer came from my older friend Jack. He was sitting beside his wife of forty years, our good friend Susie. "I've been coming to these things for decades," Jack said with a grin, "and I mostly come for the food!" Everyone laughed. There is indeed a lot of good food at a seder table.

I was already uncomfortable by this point but hadn't yet processed why. While the other Christians at the table answered the question, I was trying to find a way to leave the room gracefully. Thankfully, Sima was fussing, so I stood up with her and walked into the kitchen. I was still visible to those around the table, but now there was a convenient wall between us. I missed the third answer.

Then, I wandered to the doorway between the rooms for the fourth answer, this one from a Montessori teacher and activist, who was raised Catholic. She said, "I have little connection with my childhood faith anymore, and that's fine with me. I am a spiritual seeker and I always enjoy the seder. In fact, I probably enjoy it more than Robert, here," she explained, gesticulating to her spouse sitting beside her. He grinned, and everyone chuckled, knowing that, even though Robert was a Jew, he was also often hostile toward Judaism, its rituals and practices. "She's right about that!" he concurred.

I was the only one left to answer, and I began to inch back into the kitchen; I figured they would just move on. Clearly, I had to care for the baby and was too preoccupied with that important task to answer this little question. But Jason, who had posed it, wouldn't let it go.

"Jon, what about you? We haven't heard from you, yet," he said in full voice, reaching me through the open doorway. I shifted Sima to the other hip and took two steps back into the dining room. I was steaming by this point, and had suddenly figured out why.

I began by confessing, "To be honest, I was trying not to answer..." but then changed my tone: "because frankly, the question kind of pisses me off. I mean, it is an honest question, but it bothers me that I have to be here at this seder table *as something.* Why is that?" Everyone turned to face me, probably surprised at the rising emotion in my voice.

"Do I have to be here as a 'Christian'?" I went on. "I am married to this beautiful woman," I said, motioning toward Michal. "Together with her, we are raising our daughter as a Jew. We pray and together we follow the practices of Judaism. Yes, I am also a Catholic, but for good and for bad I have thrown in my lot with the Jewish people.

"But I'm not here wearing a sign. I'm not here tonight as a 'Christian.' There's no imprint on my chest. It is not an ontological condition. Can't I just be here as a *human being*?"

With that I took a deep breath and went to sit down. On the way to my chair, dear Susie grabbed my hand and whispered, "Yes."

It was once the case that being identified with a religious tradition was a singular form of allegiance. One had to be *this*, but also very clearly and simultaneously, *not that.* Plus, *this* came with a lot of assumptions about your religious life. If you were a Jew, you supported Israel. If Catholic, you supported the pope. A Muslim woman covered her hair. In contrast, being religiously "outside the box" has become almost normative today. Maybe the best metaphor is actually to say there is no longer a box at all, especially beyond the most traditional religious communities.

And more people than ever before have begun to add the *that*—by bringing non-native practices into their religious lives. For example, since the mid-20th century there has been an infusion of Buddhism within American Judaism. Perhaps more striking, the percentage of Jews practicing in Buddhist settings is astronomical compared to their share of the general population. The term "JewBu" was created to describe the kinship between the Buddhist worldview and meditation practices with Jewish theology and prayer. While many of these JewBus are mostly Buddhist in practice and Jewish much more superficially, these seemingly different traditions can combine seamlessly in the life of a Western Jew today, as described in Sylvia Boorstein's *That's Funny, You Don't Look Buddhist*.[5] Michal has, in fact, sat on retreat with Sylvia and describes her as simultaneously part guru, part *rebbe*, and part *bubbe* (the Yiddish terms for "rabbi" and "grandma," respectively).

Surprisingly and increasingly, some Christians are finding their religious lives being enriched by Buddhism as well. This is why Catholic theologian Paul Knitter is able to write a book titled *Without Buddha I Could Not Be a Christian*.[6] Yes, Knitter refers to himself as a Christian, but clearly his religious identity is much more complex than that word allows.

Don't misunderstand. We are not advocating syncretism (and neither does Knitter), as if there are no differences between religious paths, or as if the differences don't matter. They do matter. And while some Jews and Christians have found it is possible to integrate Eastern practice and thought into their religious lives, it remains somewhat more difficult for them to find common ground with each other's competing theologies and assumptions.

In one illustrative moment, the two of us sat uncomfortably as we were grilled in the home of board members of the Florida community that eventually rejected Michal as their potential rabbi on the grounds of Jon's religious affiliation. As uncomfortable as they were with a Catholic in their congregational mix, the board members didn't seem to find the Buddha statues scattered throughout the home where we were meeting, or the hostess's upcoming Buddhist retreat, to be paradoxical or relevant in any way.

We keep our Jewish and Christian and Yogic practices separated in our lives. Michal doesn't do "Jewish yoga"; it feels unnecessary and unhelpful to conjoin them, and yet, she's both a Jew and a yogi, and both practices enhance the sense of clarity and gratitude in her life. And Jon doesn't consider going to mass to be the same thing as *davenning* in *shul*, even though what he gets out of both practices is quite similar.

But into this new field of practicing our faiths come other interfaith couples, including ones that attempt to live, learn, and even worship actively in a hybrid form that allows simultaneous traditions to breathe. We are thinking of people like Susan Katz Miller, who has written her own memoir, *Being*

Both: Embracing Two Religions in One Interfaith Family. Raised in, and raising her children in, an interfaith household, she shares her experiences and desire to be united religiously by creating a novel, combined identity and practice.[7]

Still, combining religious traditions is not necessary in order to be spiritually connected to each other. It seems that everywhere we go we meet couples who tell us that they are joined in an interfaith relationship and retaining the particulars of their own traditions, and yet they are profoundly connected to each other both religiously and spiritually. As we explained in the introduction to this book, we certainly feel this way.

So do our new friends Leslie and Gerry. Leslie is a Conservative Jew and Gerry has been an involved Presbyterian for thirty years. They live in North Carolina. She's a lawyer-turned-nonprofit executive, and Gerry teaches philosophy to university students. As Leslie told us, she was previously married to a fellow Jew who was agnostic and religiously disengaged, "and that was a lot harder than being married to an involved Christian." Gerry challenges her to examine her faith and to live it more intentionally, and Leslie does the same for Gerry. More than that, it is obvious when you are with them that the spiritual connection they feel to each other reaches across religious boundaries.

This experience has been echoed by many of the couples we know. It seems that sharing a religiously engaged life with a religiously engaged partner of a different tradition can be significantly more satisfying than a relationship with a less engaged partner with the same background. Perhaps this is because, in reality, narrowly defined religious boundaries are not necessary requirements for living a faith.

✴ ॐ ☯ ✡ ☽ ☮

MICHAL During a recent tutoring session, a young woman in the process of preparing for her bat mitzvah explained to me that as an adopted child of a mixed marriage she wasn't sure "what she was." Her mother, on the other hand, stated that she considered herself "two-thirds Jewish." There was once a time when being Jewish was more like being pregnant, you were or you weren't. In Jewish legal terms, whether progressive or traditional, this is still the case, except that there are different benchmarks for determining whether you are in or out based on what denomination you are in.

"Who is a Jew?" has long been a question of deep importance in Jewish community, and not only so you know whom to marry or to invite for *Shabbos* dinner. There is a long tradition of looking for Jewish names on lists, whether of Oscar winners, major league baseball players, or disaster victims. Whether in the next town or across the world, this exercise was a source of connection. Nationally and worldwide, the number of Jews is carefully tracked and the results are rigorously analyzed. And contemporary culture has effectively complicated both of these processes; we miss the Jewish Smiths and O'Briens, whether created via intermarriage or conversion, and how do you count a house with one "I don't know" plus a "two-thirds"?

Progressive denominations are, in some ways, more stringent about determining who counts as a Jew than are traditional communities, which stick solely to the rule of maternity except in cases of proper, traditional conversion. Case in point: If one of my older nephews were to walk into some Reform or Reconstructionist synagogues today, he would be advised that without Jewish education and ongoing exposure to Jewish life and tradition he would not be considered a Jew. With one Jewish parent and no participation in Jewish life and education, the genetic component passed on by the mother has essentially been voided.

On the other hand, I have long joked about the possible scenario of walking with one of these same nephews down the streets of Brooklyn and passing a traditional synagogue in need of one more man to make a *minyan*. It is conceivable that a man standing in their doorway would slap a *kippah* on my nephew's head and ask him to join them and complete their quorum—so they could pray and read from the Torah. I would be left standing on the sidewalk, my female Jewishness (and rabbinate!) completely useless to them.

All this points to the second ubiquitous question asked in my religious world: "Why be Jewish?" As you may have guessed, it isn't a question that interests me much. And as we have already noted, it isn't even clear what it means to be Jewish. I am more interested in who is *doing* Jewish rather than *being* Jewish, because at least doing provides a basis of shared experience and values and not merely labels, or memory, or Jewish "pride," which I hear a lot about but frankly don't really understand.

This brings me back to my "two-thirds Jewish" mom, who is likely doing more Judaism than a bunch of her truly Jewish counterparts. Communities with growing numbers of intermarried families, which is nearly every non-Orthodox congregation these days, need to figure out how to include non-Jewish participants, many of whom are quite engaged, in ways that make sense, and the results vary. On one extreme, there are synagogues that simply make no distinctions between Jewish and non-Jewish community members, inviting everyone to take honors or lead prayers during services, although these are quite rare. On the other end of the spectrum are more traditional *shuls*, where interfaith families are still novel, which provide few opportunities for a non-Jew to participate beyond sitting in the sanctuary, perhaps as an associate member of the congregation.

Professionally, I am in a funny position as a rabbi for a movement that looks to Jewish peoplehood first and foremost, in that someone's simply being a "Member of the Tribe" doesn't excite me very much. But I heartily invite all, MOTs or not, to learn, pray, and find solace in Jewish tradition, and I am a willing guide. When it comes to discerning religious boundaries between Jews and non-Jews, I am fairly liberal but still believe that there should be "benefits to membership." Yet the contributions of the many "fellow travelers" in the communities I have served are so striking that I tend to have little discernment other than at moments around key rituals, a wedding, or lifting the Torah for the community.

Personally, the relationship with my non-Jewish husband has been the most enriching religious experience of my life.

JON I am finding more and more affinity, today, with people who feel simultaneously religiously committed and religiously amorphous. For those in such a situation, I suspect it is often because we have come out of a tradition where believing is king.

Traditional Protestantism teaches what the New Testament clearly says on a few occasions: salvation comes through faith, and faith equals belief. The man who basically codified the Protestant mind-set, Martin Luther, said that it was a verse in Romans chapter 1 that caused a revolution in his thinking about religion: "the one who is righteous will live by faith" (Romans 1:17). And so, belief became sovereign. The foundation of Protestantism became (1) knowing the basic principles of faith, and (2) stating them as convictions, like a form of allegiance. That's all you need to be a follower of Christ, a "Christian."

But believing comes and goes, doesn't it? Believing is a state of mind. The traditional Protestant way had me thinking that believing, all by itself, was transformative. The thoughts in my head quite literally made me a different (ontological) being than others who failed to have those thoughts. Thoughts therefore "saved" me—just in my thinking them and saying them out loud. How frightened I was, then, when it felt impossible to constantly maintain the correct state of mind—let alone the most appropriately spoken words!

Thankfully, those days are gone, as they are for many of my contemporaries. We have come to understand that belief is transient, and also that belief is far less important than practice. If I want to understand someone's religious life, I don't ask them what they believe, but what they do.

Ludwig Wittgenstein, a 20th-century philosopher famous for critiquing imprecise language and thought, often reflected on religious life and belief. The most important thing he ever said on the subject was probably this: "You can't argue with the form of a life." In other words, religious belief may be imprecise, and often unsupportable on purely rational grounds, but what religion most essentially does is mold or shape a person for good. Something not to be argued with.

That's why I go to mass. That is, in fact, why I have done many unquantifiable religious things over the years, from praying with rosary beads to going to confession to helping homeless people: not out of obligation, not because I know or can comprehend what are the effects and results of the doing, but simply because I feel I should, and I seek to be formed by my religious tradition. Even when I can't explain precisely why. I even kneel as I enter and leave church; what a crazy and irrational thing that is.

Today I see it this way: thinking is seriously important in a religious and spiritual life, but not belief. Belief is only one result of thought, and in my experience, belief can actually suspend thinking. Probing, struggling, even arguing with God, and the texts of our traditions, is honoring to God in ways that I used to understand only belief to be. As Thomas Aquinas once said, "The more we probe for God, the closer we come." Or, as the poet William Butler Yeats wrote in one of his best poems: "God guard me from those thoughts men think / In the mind alone; / He that sings a lasting song / Thinks in a marrow-bone" ("A Prayer for Old Age").

For these reasons, I readily call myself a Catholic. Every faith is a way of relativizing God, and to be a Catholic is to identify myself with a tradition, a liturgy, and a group of people down through history. I am (mostly) proud to do that—and to call myself Catholic. I hesitate to claim, however, the label "Christian," because it always seems to come out sounding like I am this instead of that. Christian identity is not, as

I said at that seder table, an ontological condition. (Of course, there are millions of Christians who believe that it is; I just don't happen to be one of them.) I cannot believe anything in my brain, or say anything with my mouth, that makes me less or more of a person than you.

So, if you were to ask me, *What do you believe?* my answer would likely be, "I don't always know." Or, "It can change—what I believe—from one day to the next." Or, most likely, "I don't think it matters a lot what I believe, because my current state of mind does not define, or give much meaning, to my spiritual life or my religious convictions." Please ask me what I do, instead. Ask me about the form of my life.

Every one of us has to answer that basic question: What is the form of your life? In other words, what matters to you? Who are you?

Whether you are more spiritual than religious, a hyphenated combination of traditions, confident in your identity as one of the "nones," or morphing and transitioning from one of these categories to any number of others, we are all in the same boat of having to figure it out, find our way, and make our lives ones that matter. And we all encounter those from many other paths, whether as friends, family, colleagues, or, yes, romantic partners. Cultivating an understanding of ourselves as well as an openness to understanding each other, and doing so consciously and reflectively, could not be more important.

PART II

Coming Together

Each of us enters our relationships bringing unique experiences and a significant past. Some of us have religious histories from which we are attempting to "recover." Others have ones they are proud of. We can check similar boxes for our romantic histories, for celebrating what we learned or mourning why we failed. And then there's a whole lot in between. We all bring all of this to each new relationship. We, Jon and Michal, will share a glimpse into our own relational baggage with you, here.

Then, you meet someone special and try to fit all of these pieces together into a new puzzle. It may turn out that despite great compatibility, those pieces marked "faith traditions" don't necessarily match up. But you start to date, and eventually find yourself telling your parents, family members, children, and friends that you are partnering with a person of another faith. Perhaps you decide to marry and need to figure out what that would look like. Or decide not to marry, and determine how that would work. These are all challenges to be faced—and opportunities to mark who we are today, religiously and spiritually, as individuals and couples and eventually, perhaps, families.

CHAPTER 4

—

Getting to Know You

Nearly two decades ago a twenty-one-year-old Christian named Joshua Harris wrote a book that quickly became a bestseller among conservative evangelicals called *I Kissed Dating Goodbye*.[8] He argued that for Christians to be faithful to the purity demanded of them by God, they should "court" in group situations, with the encouragement and active participation of their parents, rather than "date" one-on-one. Harris was urging Christian teenagers and college students (for that's the audience—they marry young, remember) to avoid situations where romance can develop before marriage.

Harris taught them that they shouldn't, in fact, pursue romance at all. His book struck a chord and sold a million copies, largely because that chord has been played for centuries by those who believe that dating should only exist as a careful test for marriage compatibility. Privacy, according to this view, is inappropriate before marriage, and one's community, congregation, and family provide a young man or woman with the truest tests for love over infatuation.

These "courtship" advocates encourage dating to take place only in communal settings, an idea they share with traditionalists from other religions as well. A Muslim family in Lehore, a Sikh family in East London, and a Mormon family in Utah may all agree that dating, as it's commonly done today, is too individualistic and focuses too much on the couple by themselves. Instead, they encourage couples to get to know each other while surrounded by extended family. These families are also sometimes bound together by shared ethnic identities, as when the couple in London is not only Sikh, but lives in an Indian enclave, or, in this country, when a couple may identify as much or more with being Polish or Italian, et cetera, as they do with being Catholic. In all of these examples, this is likely how the couple's life will be lived, should they marry: surrounded by family. Moving out of state, across the country, or even out of the neighborhood is almost unthinkable.

American religious historian Lauren Winner has argued that dating as we know it—the sort of one-on-one getting to know each other—has only existed since the early 20th century, when the invention of the automobile made it possible. Otherwise, in the history of human relationships, communities and extended families were always the primary context in which couples courted, shining a light on how contemporary dating is overly romanticized, individualistic, and driven by sometimes illusory emotions.[9]

There are other religious conservatives who dislike the "courtship" teaching of their co-religionists, at least in some cases. This view, they argue, doesn't work for older singles, or for those who live far from family or have non-Christian parents. Mega-church pastors Matt Chandler (in Dallas–Ft. Worth, with 10,000 members) and Mark Driscoll (in Seattle, with similar numbers) hold this view.[10] Their focus is to teach singles how to date "righteously" as they find Christian mates. They make an individual's faith the number one priority, and encourage each person to find a partner equally strong in belief; neither family nor community need interfere and geography need not limit possibilities.

This approach dovetails well with the reality of 21st-century life where friendships and relationships begin, or sometimes occur entirely, in cyberspace. What started decades ago as personal ads, and yes, Michal remembers her first in 1988, has swelled to include hundreds of online dating sites—some generic, some incredibly specific to particular orientations, religions, values, or hobbies. The universe is now most truly one's neighborhood, if one wants it to be.

In conservative Islam, sheiks explain to young Muslims that marriage is good, God's first intention for all. The popular dating website SingleMuslim.com started in the UK, more recently expanded into the United States at us.SingleMuslim.com, is evidence of this. With millions of active members, each apparently seeking a *shaadi* (wedding) through "marriage introduction," the us.SingleMuslim .com website explains that they are a real alternative to traditional, arranged Muslim marriages throughout the world; and the site "provides the best possible help for our brothers and sisters to find their ideal Muslim marriage partner and complete their faith within a happy and successful Islamic marriage."

Jews also have resources in cyberspace to meet their match.

"Saw You at Sinai" caters to religious Jewish singles and features matchmakers who provide links to specific profiles and manage the process of communicating with and eventually meeting a potential partner. JDate provides searching using a wide range of affiliation and levels of religious observance. For example, one Conservative Jew can meet another, both of whom keep kosher, and so on. Similarly, every spiritual expression seems to have a dating site these days. The site DharmaMatch.com uses this for a marketing slogan: "We understand that your beliefs, values, and spirituality are important to you, and we believe that these are things which shouldn't be sacrificed when seeking relationships." And then there's everything from PresbyterianSingles.com to WiccanPassions.com to a site for Mormons, LDSsingles.com, with more than 500,000 profiles and a bold quote from the Book of Mormon (and the Gospel of Matthew) at the top: "Seek, and ye shall find." No one seems to be claiming that a spouse is what Jesus was encouraging people to find, but the quote works.

Most conservative clergy, across the traditions, are also often outspoken on another topic that affects who and how we date, and clearly sets conservatives and progressives cleanly apart today: gender roles. Joshua Harris is, in fact, a prominent member of the Council on Biblical Manhood and Womanhood (CBMW), an evangelical 501(c)(3) organization whose stated mission "is to set forth the teachings of the Bible about the complementary differences between men and women, created equally in the image of God, because these teachings are essential for obedience to Scripture and for the health of the family and the church." Needless to say, in such a worldview, there's no room for LGBT folks, dating web-sites like RainbowChristians.com and GayChristiansDating .com, gay marriage, or perhaps even a stay-at-home dad.

Dating, sexuality, and gender are all topics Christian conservatives, the CBMW, and similarly minded groups often resonate with values expressed by traditional ethnic communities that are not necessarily religious. One thinks of Latino families—particularly a half generation ago—who shared a subculture in which adjectives like "macho" and "machismo" were not pejoratives, but qualities desired by males if they wanted to be accepted by others. Gender roles were nearly always clearly defined and static, and heterosexuality was the only accepted norm. Thankfully, today these attitudes and assumptions are beginning to change.

Of course messages about dating are first transmitted in religious supplementary schools or parochial schools or by parents who clearly prefer their kids play with friends from church, well before one may be seriously thinking about dating. Across religions and denominations, programs for teens or pre-teens likely incorporate a sexual ethics component that will touch upon dating and, explicitly or implicitly, address the specific topic of interfaith dating. A generation ago, for instance, you could assume that in most every synagogue, whether it is more conservative or more liberal, the message delivered was that dating a non-Jew is a problem.

But in this century, there are many Jewish settings where this message no longer works. This was certainly the case for Michal's synagogue in Vermont, where the majority of her flock was interfaith families. A colleague of Michal's in

New Hampshire with a similar demographic once described an effective session with his eighth-grade cohort: the class discussed the Sholom Aleichem story about Chava, Tevye's middle daughter. The story had much more detail about this young woman, her personality, and her relationship with her father than was portrayed in *Fiddler on the Roof*, but ultimately was about her marriage to the young Russian and her consequent rejection by her father. The teacher of the class was herself intermarried. The conversation that ensued certainly had more subtlety than could have been imagined in other settings and eras.

Today, the messages that Jewish kids hear in religious schools are a function of the synagogue, vis-à-vis denominational affiliation and even geographical location. The membership of a Reform synagogue in Los Angeles likely looks rather different from one in Los Alamos. And those Reform congregations have different priorities and make different assumptions than Conservative or Orthodox ones. Explaining that dating a non-Jew is a problem in some way doesn't play well to a roomful of fourteen-year-olds of which over half have a non-Jewish parent. What teenager, dutifully sitting in *shul*, is willing to hear a rabbi, or anyone else, explain that her or his own parent simply isn't a good match?! Furthermore, one can assume at least one of those kids has two moms or two dads. Traditional religious assumptions don't serve the reality of 21st-century family life.

With the growing diversity of religious and relational life, it is only appropriate that there are now so many approaches to, and options for, meeting a potential mate. But websites, speed dating, and singles parties are great only when you are purposefully and consciously seeking a partner. What happens more often is that we meet people in our ordinary daily lives. How many meet and marry a coworker, a waiter at their favorite restaurant, or their best friend's brother? These relationships start when we might not be looking, and without the boundaries we create in a personal profile.

For example, our friend Lucy first met Nick one afternoon when he was, in her words, "The weird guy who rollerbladed into the coffee shop where I was a barista." She was a Jewish college student; he was a Christian townie. The next time he came into the shop, Nick asked Lucy out, and two years later, they married. Other friends of ours, Stacy and Mark, met at a Laundromat where they shyly caught each other's eyes over the edges of their respective books, not so unlike how Chava and Fyedka met in *Fiddler*. Now married with a child, they still find they like being together doing parallel, quiet, solo activities. Lainie and Phillip met through an interest in science fiction; Rachel and Jeremy both played Celtic music. Many different aspects of our lives bring us together.

Of course, most people don't go looking for religious complications in their relationships. Seeking love is tough enough without that—or the accompanying politics. But when we meet someone by chance and begin dating and getting to know them, coming from different faith traditions adds another layer of complexity. So while one may not use religious difference as a boundary to forming relationships, failing to address the issue specifically can still create future problems. For any couple interested in spiritual life, it seems prudent to ask: How will we build a life together, even,

or perhaps especially, when we come from different backgrounds or have different levels of interest in religious life?
Time is well spent working this out early in a relationship,
right along with the other most basic questions of personal
values, how and where to live, whether to start a family,
attitudes about money, career, and life balance.

As two people whose lives revolve around religion—
intellectually, spiritually, practically, professionally—our
own religious lives were evident and active throughout our
friendship, relationship, and ultimately, our marriage. And
as our backgrounds were so different, we had a lot of work
to do to really understand each other's religious and spiritual approaches, needs, and priorities. But for us, discussing religion was a natural part of being together, and rarely,
especially early in our relationship, did it feel like convers-
ing about an "issue." And of course, we still had the myriad
other details to discover about each other that would determine whether we were truly compatible.

JON "I'm not sure if you'd actually call it a 'date,' but I'm
having a glass of wine with someone, tonight," I mentioned
to my parents on the phone one afternoon in early February,
just before we were about to hang up.

"*Really?*" mom replied, showing a little too much interest
in her voice.

"Uh huh," I said.

"Who is it?" she asked.

"The rabbi in town."

Then my dad spoke up. "Jon...we are talking about a *woman...right?*" My father sometimes thinks he doesn't know me at all; I've changed in so many ways since I left home.

"Yes, Dad," I said. Then I explained that her name was Michal Woll, we'd met once or twice before, and I'd heard that she was going to be leaving the synagogue in Woodstock. I had some experience with one of Michal's principal, soon-to-be-former, employers, since the founding president of the synagogue had also once been my employer and friend at a Vermont publishing house. A tough man to work for, I knew, and without knowing any details of Michal's situation, I figured that a personality clash may have had something to do with what was going on. "May I buy you a glass of wine?" I asked her via e-mail.

"Well, a glass of wine sounds like fun," my mother said as we hung up.

It didn't really seem like a date, although I was interested enough in Michal to send a query in the first place. And I'd been interested enough to listen carefully when her name came up in others' conversations, as names do when one lives in a small New England village.

We first met a year earlier, in February 2008, when I was separated and sharing a house with my Episcopal priest, Christina, her husband, also a priest, and son. My two teenage kids would come back and forth, splitting their time equally with me and my soon-to-be ex-wife. When marriages end, even when they are mostly unhappy ones, it sucks. Dividing property, meeting with lawyers, stressing out the kids, quibbling over assets and debts, trying to be honest and yet not necessarily bad-mouthing each other—it is all so unpleasant. It was a difficult time for me. I was glad to be living with friends.

And I was pleased that Christina invited me that day in February when her clergy group was coming around for lunch. "You should give them a copy of your new book," she suggested, meaning *Almost Catholic*, one that I'd recently preached about in church. I liked the idea of giving away a book to clergy who might actually read it, but I couldn't see that a Mennonite, a Unitarian-Universalist, and a rabbi were necessarily the right audience for that particular one—so I grabbed copies of an earlier work that was truly multi-faith.

The lunch was largely unremarkable, but meeting Michal stuck with me. I had first seen her, but we hadn't met, six months earlier, in her first month as the new rabbi in Woodstock, when I visited the *shul*. The choir from my church was participating in an ecumenical liturgical concert, and I stayed afterward for the evening service. She was beautiful, and I don't mean just physically; as she led the congregation in prayer and worship, I remember thinking that she shined. Which is probably why, the day after that clergy group lunch, while standing in the kitchen, I remember tentatively saying to Christina, "You know, I think I could date again. Michal is interesting, isn't she?"

The following month, she showed up at my church, sitting in the pews on a Sunday morning, and I noticed her immediately. The simple fact that she was there impressed me. Most people don't take the time or have enough interest to experience the religious rituals of another. At coffee hour afterward I encouraged my daughter to join me in saying hello. "She's the rabbi in town," I explained, wanting to see her again and also wanting Clelia to know more professional women.

But that was all. Over the next year, divorcing took most of my emotional energy. What was left was spent with my children. And my work life was plenty full, what with my usual publishing duties as well as writing two books, both of which (gladly) required short research trips with a friend to Europe. Life was full. Dating felt entirely optional.

And then there was the idea in my head that I wasn't meant to date. I was clearly a failure at relationships for having remained in a failing one for so long, and because I now wore the scarlet letter of "the divorced." I prayed about all of this, in church and out; I asked for forgiveness for whatever was my fault, not knowing exactly what was and what wasn't; and in all I was not so much asking God what to do—because that's never really been my way of communicating with God—but sitting in silence just listening. Nothing really came. I took several trips to two monasteries, in Georgia and nearby Massachusetts, for spiritual retreats, sitting for hours and chatting with monks who had, by that time, become friends. I felt comforted, but that was all. Each time I returned, I went out of my way to tell friends that I had zero interest in ever marrying again.

I felt my situation begin to change on the second of January 2009. That was the day my lawyer called to say that we finally had a schedule for concluding the divorce. It would require a few meetings, a little more haggling, and was I ready for all of that, she asked. I hung up the phone and decided that the year beginning needed to be about more than this unpleasantness, and I resolved to do two things: open myself to new friendships and lose some weight. Over the last decade of overworking and being unhappy at home, I'd eaten to feel better and gained a lot of weight. I was tubby. So I turned to the ascetic teachings of the monks I loved and decided to stop eating unless necessary, and to eat little or nothing that I actually enjoyed, until I'd lost one hundred pounds. It was the following month that Michal and I got together for that glass of wine. Connecting with her felt very much a part of my process of renewal.

Throughout the late winter and spring, we started getting together a couple of times a month. I asked Michal if she would like to do something, and we had dinner at one of the local inns. Two weeks later we went to a movie. I asked questions about her Judaism, and she asked about my Christianity. On spiritual matters we seemed to really gel. We talked about how we disliked stuff and valued serious friendships. She pushed me to explain what I feel when I go to church, as well as my relationship to Jesus. There were differences between us, to be sure, but the more time we spent together, it became clear how much we had in common.

Then, we went to the movies again, this time to see Sean Penn play Harvey Milk, and I think that is the night when I fell in love with her. We weren't even holding hands with each other by that point, but as I sat beside Michal I could feel her presence. And when Josh Brolin (playing Dan White) shot Penn/Milk, murdering him in cold blood, assassination-style, Michal leaped at least twelve inches out of her chair, as if she was herself absorbing the bullet. I sat there intently, but motionless.

This was about the time when, one afternoon, I took a close look around my new apartment rethinking the religious art and objects on the walls. Michal was coming over for dinner the next day. I'd accumulated many things over the years, some precious to me, others less so. One of these was a large, wooden crucifix, a replica of the one that hung in the church of San Damiano in Assisi, from which St. Francis first heard God "speak" to him. I considered, sadly, how the primary symbol of my tradition has also been the ugliest symbol of oppression of Michal's tradition. I took down the crucifix. A few months later I would donate it to a community of Sisters of St. Clare in Boston, with whom I had a relationship.

We had become close confidantes and began talking about other relationships. I told Michal about a flirtatious evening I spent with an author/friend while out of town, and she told me about upcoming plans to spend time with a rabbi in New York whom a friend had told her she should meet. Upon returning from that weekend trip, I heard all about the time she spent with him, and how he was planning on visiting Vermont in a few weeks. A few weekends later, despite the fact that Michal and I had no commitment to each other, I recall walking past her house to have a look, seeing the car with New York plates, and seething.

By June, as we sat in her living room one evening, I asked a question that had been on my mind for a while. "Are we dating?" I said. Not having much experience in dating over the last two decades, I wasn't quite sure if platonic dinners, walks, movies, and interesting conversations rated. She assured me that we were not. Disappointed, I still knew that this was a relationship that mattered—and that mattered to me. So we continued to spend regular time together, and I figured that if she ever wanted to return to that question, I would be happy to.

MICHAL I was never sure whether to be more surprised by how difficult it was to arrange a get-together with the other local liberal clergy or that we managed to align our calendars once a month at all. There had never been a rabbi in town before, and the addition of one created a critical mass of four. In the week prior to our confirmed February 2008 get-together I received an e-mail from the Episcopal priest:

> Dear Colleagues,
>   I am looking forward to hosting our monthly gathering. A lovely young man has moved into my house. He writes and publishes religious books and works from our home. I was hoping we could invite him to our lunch next week. I think he'd be an interesting addition to our little group.

Of course none of us objected to an infusion of ideas or energy, or to meeting a like-minded soul whose professional life was immersed in religion. Indeed, when we arrived at Christina's big, old, federal-style home, big enough for her three and Jon's three more, we were greeted by Christina and a large, dark-haired man with a goatee and a resonant voice.

We chatted in the front library and sat down to lunch of soup and salad. Alongside each plate was a copy of a book Jon had written. *Praying with Our Hands*, which beautifully illustrated how hand gestures are used devotionally across world religions, was a nice choice for our diverse group, but the gifting felt awkward. Certainly by the time lunch ended I knew about our connection through his previous work with the local Jewish publishing house and my new position at the synagogue, but the details of the gathering are a blur.

A few weeks later I went to hear Christina preach and saw Jon at the coffee hour afterward. He was joined by his teenage daughter, who made no effort to mask her disinterest in being there. But I didn't linger, feeling very much the stranger in a strange land.

Almost a year to the day since we first met we saw each other again, at a screening of *The Curious Case of Benjamin Button* at our little town hall theater. I was with some women from synagogue; he was again accompanied by his daughter. We recognized each other, nodded, waved. The e-mail the next morning caught me off guard:

> Dear Michal,
>
>   I hope you enjoyed the film last night. It is a remarkable one for many reasons, I think. I wanted to send a quick note to say that I heard about what has happened at the synagogue, and I'd enjoy getting together to talk sometime, if you would like to. Perhaps I could meet you for a glass of wine some evening?
>
> Peace, Jon

After a round or two of negotiations we ended up at the tavern of a local inn later that week, where I actually had a beer. Jon sipped his house red and explained that he had a good sense of what my experience may have been like; I was working with some people he knew quite well. What had "happened" was that the *shul* did not renew my contract and I would be ending my tenure there soon. Had they offered one it would have been a difficult negotiation to create conditions under which I would have stayed.

The topic of conversation transitioned from my professional experience to his, to his marriage, then to mine. It was a comfortable exchange. We parted and walked back to our respective homes, each a few blocks from the inn, in opposite directions, both bundled up against a very cold winter's evening. After some months at Christina's, Jon had moved to an apartment in the village.

Jon followed up, invited me to dinner the following week, during which he was embarrassed that his daughter, needing to get out of the house, called him and asked to join us. But I loved having Clelia with us for coffee. They were planning a college visit trip to California, and Jon sent me regular updates of their activities, which I found surprising. But once he returned we settled into a regular routine of a meal or a film every week or two.

I was enjoying Jon's company but not necessarily attracted. He was heavy and had a bit of an air about him, all in all, just a little too "big" for my sensitive, and active, nature. But Jon seemed responsive to my lifestyle and needs, was careful about not offending me when we would go out and eat, thinking I kept kosher but learning I was a vegetarian. There was always something interesting to talk about. He loved ideas, music, and culture. He liked to learn, didn't mind learning from me, and had a lot to teach. He was a classics major, the thinker; I was an engineer, practical. The contrast was interesting. And over time, things between us seemed to shift.

Religion remained at the center of our conversations, just as it was at the center of our individual lives. We shared our journeys as religious seekers, even as those paths were so different. How we fit or didn't fit within our families. Of course Jon had worked in Jewish publishing for years and knew a lot about Judaism and Jewish culture, and he knew a lot of Jews, mostly well-known ones for whom he edited books. We shared an appreciation for Eastern thought, a disdain for New Age fluff, and a combination of deep knowledge, reverence, and a bit of cynicism about our respective traditions. In some ways he was *more* culturally Jewish than I was, with his interest in Jewish books, weekly reading of the Arts section of my Jewish *Forward* newspaper, and being able to quote most episodes of *Seinfeld*, of which I knew only "The Big Salad."

Jon was clear about his intentions to remain single. Sitting in a wing chair in my living room, he explained that he would love to be in a long-term relationship someday but had no thoughts of getting married again. He'd remained in a bad marriage for over a decade and now, looking to become Catholic, divorce and remarriage was complicated.

Eventually, a mutual friend divulged what else was happening during these months. While I was describing to her something Jon had shared about Clelia's losing weight, Laura exclaimed, "Jon's also doing great!" I then realized that over the past months Jon was literally shrinking before my eyes.

Still, we seemed like buddies, escorting each other through recoveries from bad marriages and bad jobs. And I felt completely at home, and completely myself, with him.

"Are we dating?" It was mid-June. Jon was in my kitchen, chatting one evening.

"I don't think so. I think we are hanging out."

"Really? I think we might be dating."

"Well, you don't really act like we are dating. You don't walk me home from the movies, let alone ask to come in. You've never tried to hold my hand. No, we seem to be hanging out."

In the midst of this repartee my phone rang. I let the machine pick up only to hear a congregant leave an awful message: "Jake Horner died. He is at home." Within minutes the phone rang again. It was the mother of the young man I had just heard about. I once again let it ring through, using the time to collect my thoughts and wits. Jon and I said goodbye, and I turned to address this huge tragedy in my small community.

I don't remember whether I processed much about the death with Jon, but once we reconnected after the funeral it was clear that something had shifted, and that if it was to shift further I was going to have to be the one to invite it or make it happen.

Over all of these months I had spent little time at Jon's place, an apartment that he wasn't very excited about but had room for the kids and was affordable, which wasn't easy in our upscale village. But one warm spring evening I visited, carrying a bottle of white wine, and Jon sparked something in me, mirroring something about myself that felt somewhat unusual and often left me feeling a bit lonely. "I don't have time, or patience, for acquaintances. I want deep relationships, friendships that mean something." I could name that tune. And that confession gave me even more permission to make this connection more personal.

Finally, sitting in my living room watching a movie one evening, I slid over close and put my head on Jon's shoulder, which I had been aching to do a week earlier while in the exact same situation at his place. Eventually he kissed me, lifted his head and asked, "Should we go upstairs?"

"No. We shouldn't." Jon has since reminded me that he asked a second time, only to get rebuffed again. But with as much time as we had spent together and as close as we were, much of the "getting to know you" of dating was already done, and things moved quickly.

This transition shifted the nature of our interaction around religion, but only slightly. We continued to banter about our different theologies. Jon, even in his liberalism, could not let go of a personal God. I rejected that for a more Eastern, karmic interpretation of God's response to my doings in the world. Then, being perhaps more typical than I like to admit, the one issue that unsettled me was, yes, you guessed it: Jesus. What about Jesus? What did Jon believe about Jesus? I know I was hoping for the classic, modern, progressive response: a teacher, a rabbi, of mythic proportions.

One evening as we were cleaning up from dinner I asked the question. Jon sat at the kitchen island and said, "Jesus is just all right with me." I let the answer hang there, feeling a bit rebuffed, but enjoying the shared reference to, and appreciation of, music from our youth. As time went on and our relationship deepened, I began to understand what that response meant to Jon, and it was all right with me, too.

CHAPTER 5

Got Commitment?

We'd all like it to be as simple as falling in love. *I love you, so what else matters?* On the other hand, actual love can be hard to find, so when potential barriers get in the way we might attempt to talk ourselves out of it: *I love you, but...* We have probably all had one or both of these conversations in our relationships.

We went through this process, and it's in this chapter that we discuss our own individual deliberating about each other, right through the evening of the proposal itself, the hesitations that were renewed at that moment ("Maybe...") the discussions afterward ("Impossible!") and, eventually, the "Yes."

What would commitment mean for the two of us? Sorting out this question is more difficult when religious variables are introduced. To get serious with a person of a different faith, particularly if you are both *actually serious* about faith, and deciding to commit can be tricky.

In considering a future together, we had to deliberately

discuss countless issues that had come up casually, unconsciously, or hypothetically in the months prior: housing, raising children, religion in the home, religion out of the home, our careers, work/life balance, our values around money, family, food; the list goes on and on. Committing to each other would mean far more than enjoying each other's company. Commitment does not have to mean marriage, and these issues stand for any couple desiring to forge an intimate long-term relationship.

Of course, only a fraction of that list is there solely based on our religious differences. Every couple needs to work through these issues. And we suspect that perhaps *none* of them are unique to an interfaith partnership. For example, a good friend of ours recently described one of his private worries from a quarter century ago, before committing to his wife: "But she's SO Jewish!" Both Jewish, they still had to work out how, when, and even where religion would be part of their family's life. So unless a couple meets in the context of a truly shared religious path, religion and spirituality are factors that must be addressed.

Our experience tells us that the best scenario for two people on different religious or spiritual journeys wishing to commit to each other is that they share progressive views of their faith and tradition. If one partner believes her tradition to be the one and only way, any true partnership will be nearly impossible. Surely, then, the relationship can survive only if the other partner is without any serious religious commitments of his or her own.

There will always be those who look on this view with cynicism. We've heard it firsthand. They will survey the two partners, each committed to progressive values, and say, "They must not really believe anything, so their commitment to their traditions has no real importance to them." We are not the only couple who sees this otherwise. Our friends Rachel and Jeremy, for instance, met in their thirties after Rachel had already been married and divorced. She's an involved mainline Protestant, while Jeremy's an active Conservative Jew. She remembers, post-divorce, praying to God and asking to meet a spiritual man this time around. Then, she met and fell in love with Jeremy. "I guess I should have been more specific!" she says playfully. Meanwhile, Jeremy was ending an unsatisfying relationship with a fellow Jew, one who was uninterested in his religious commitments and personal values. The new relationship moved quickly.

And then there are our friends Lainie and Phillip—she was raised Catholic and became primarily a practitioner of earth-based, or pagan, religion, and Phillip was raised a Unitarian-Universalist and still remains involved in that tradition. Lainie and Michal met when they were both new, older moms, but on each visit, their conversations about breast milk or sleep schedules quickly transitioned to ones about spirit and mystery. These accompanied them on long walks in the Vermont woods, infants strapped on their backs.

A more common scenario is one that has been referred to as "interfaithless" marriage, a union of individuals from different religious backgrounds, neither of whom have any ongoing religious commitment. These stories are well documented in a number of books that describe couples negotiating around a wedding ceremony and winter holidays who otherwise have no religious engagement. Two of Michal's three sisters entered such unions.

In the forefront of our minds through all of this was what may also be animating you. Perhaps this is even what drew you to pick up *Mixed-Up Love* in the first place: the real or anticipated challenges of others. We all have to reconcile our desires to make a relationship commitment that we imagine will be challenging for our families, colleagues, employers, congregations, friends, and sometimes even strangers.

These challenges are not always bad. Sometimes they're necessary. If we are sure and clear about our situations, we should be willing to be challenged and able to articulate an honest answer to an earnest question. Understand that there are old cultural and religious barriers that often exist for interfaith matches. Serious questions from loved ones and friends can be reasonable and justified, about many aspects of your choice of partner, not just the fact of being in an interfaith relationship.

This advice does not help much in the face of the old perspective of just saying "no" to interfaith relationships altogether. Saying "no" can be institutional or familial, with either the hierarchy of our religious tradition standing firmly in the way, or our family doing the same. There are plenty of examples of this today, from the absurd and missionary to the somewhat more reasonable. Decades ago, Michal stumbled across a small volume titled *How to Stop an Intermarriage* written in the seventies by a rabbi intent on stopping the intermarriage trend. The book was full of techniques for breaking up a couple against their will, and it has been recently reissued as *How to Prevent an Intermarriage: A Guide for Parents to Prevent Broken Hearts*, complete with a new introduction.

In considering committing to someone of another faith, it is important to recognize that some traditions simply will not allow it. This is one of the primary reasons, for instance, why there are tens of millions of former Roman Catholics in the United States: they were not allowed to marry their chosen partner in the Catholic Church, and so they up and left. In fact, in many religious traditions, including Catholicism, Jehovah's Witnesses, Buddhism, and many Protestant Christian denominations, one-third or more of those who are initiated into the tradition later leave it: "If you won't accept my chosen partner on his merits...if you won't see, as I do, how perfect she is for me as is...then I choose him— even if it means leaving *you*."

Some religious people opposed to your union may take a more missionary approach. *Winning Him Without Words*, for instance, is a popular guide for evangelical Christians to quietly hope and pray that their partners will one day become evangelical Christians, too. The authors, two women, introduce themselves this way: "Hi! We're Dineen Miller and Lynn Donovan. We are ordinary women and ordinary wives just like you. And, just like you, we believe that Jesus is the Son of God and our redeemer. Our husbands do not."[11]

Their book points to a common way to remove the barriers of being in an interfaith relationship by having one partner convert. In prior generations, the most common conversion scenario is a woman converting to Judaism, often to a somewhat uninvolved Jewish man, in order to marry.

Sometimes these conversions create an "intra-faithless" family of two uninvolved Jews. In myriad interviews she conducted for a book about interfaith marriage, Jane Kaplan discovered that these "conversions for marriage" caused the highest level of stress and divorce among all the couples she met.[12] But it is also not uncommon to find that the woman soon becomes interested and involved, increasingly so with the introduction of children into the family. This dynamic is actually often true even when the woman does *not* convert, often pushing her spouse and family to deeper involvement than he ever imagined.

The [London] *Spectator* ran a feature article in 2012 titled "Till faith do us part" about the trend of Christian women converting to Islam in order to marry Muslim men. The writer's name was Melissa Kite, and she clearly found this trend disconcerting. Citing a recent study that says that in Britain more than five thousand people a year are converting to Islam, and 62 percent of those converts are women, she began:

> A girlfriend who was about to get married was telling me about her wedding plans recently when she said, almost as an aside: "Oh, and I've converted to Islam."
>
> Her fiancé was a Muslim but she thought it no more than a minor detail—like ordering the corsages, or finalising the table plan—to arrange a private ceremony before the big day in which she took on his faith. I think she expected me to say "How lovely. And have you decided on the

centre-pieces?" But instead I blurted out: "You've done what?"[13]

Her friend goes on to explain that there is nothing really lost in her converting from her nominal Anglican faith (still the state religion in England) to Islam, because she—the girlfriend—never engaged with her Christianity, and she doesn't foresee needing to engage with Islam, either. "I don't have to wear a veil or go to mosque or anything," she tells Melissa. "It doesn't make any difference to me either way."

It's true that converting to Islam is remarkably easy compared to Judaism and Catholicism. To become a Muslim is similar to becoming a born-again Christian in the sense that it requires only a verbal statement to get the ball rolling. Both evangelical Christians and Muslims make it so easy to convert that you can even do it by yourself at home. You don't need anyone's permission to do it. Evangelicals usually call this "asking Jesus into your heart." For Muslims it is the *shahada*, an Arabic verb that means "to witness," which says, "There is no god but God; Muhammad is the messenger of God," and is ideally spoken in Arabic in order to take full effect. For a "none" marrying a person of faith this may work fine. But that's not the answer for couples who are involved in, or passionate about, their religious traditions.

Commitment in relationships has changed, just as commitment in religion has changed versus a generation or two ago. We engage with these changes in ways that are at times uncomfortable, and at others, challenging. We think of three friends and colleagues with whom we've sat and discussed these issues in recent months. First, Dr.

Philip Amerson, president of Garrett-Evangelical Theological Seminary, who, after years of pastoral life, realized that he needed to be more thoughtful and discerning in choosing to work with interfaith couples, encouraging them to move into marriage with clear expectations and plans for themselves and their families. Eboo Patel, a Muslim professional and writer, is delighted that his interfaith nonprofit's mission includes no advice-giving to the youth in his program on matters of dating or relationships. And Father Bob Oldershaw, the retired parish priest of St. Nicholas Church in Evanston, Illinois, is known for his progressive values and "pushing the envelope" in his tradition. We asked Father Bob, "How progressive are you compared to the broader Catholic world?" He answered, "When I was the pastor at St. Nick's, we were known as 'St. Nick's on thin ice.' You go out on the edge and sometimes you fall in."

Perhaps that's all of us—out on the edge—committing to, or supporting others in, interfaith relationships. While love is what draws us to our partners, just as it drew our grandparents to each other, religion is an additional realm that can challenge us. But perhaps, as in our case, your engagement in religious and spiritual life will transform from a challenge to your relationship to a source of inspiration and connection, to each other and to broader community.

JON I was confused about relationships when I met Michal. After my divorce, I was telling friends I was planning on dating but not committing to someone. "Those days are past," I would say, and I meant it religiously. Old paradigms had crumbled. But then, as sometimes happens, meeting someone can change things, and something new was being born inside of me. Michal reached me as a different person from the one I'd been before, and getting to know her removed much of the caution I had built up. Before long the line from *When Harry Met Sally* came to mind: "When you realize you want to spend the rest of your life with somebody, you want the rest of your life to start as soon as possible." Even if I didn't know how it might work.

It took about a month for Michal to respond in the affirmative to my question about dating. And it was an easy transition since we had never stopped spending time together. We continued to talk about religion. From the start, it was as if we were testing the waters to see if dating would be possible. She knew that I was in the process of converting to Catholicism and asked me why. I would explain what drew me to the Catholic Church—the strong tradition of justice and option for the poor, the beauty of ritual, emphasis on the love of God, the communion of saints, and the ways that good Catholics have always tried to revalue the past. Michal would occasionally point to parallels with Reconstructionist Judaism, which I began to deeply appreciate. I felt like I was, or could be, if it existed, a Reconstructionist Catholic/Christian. We talked about our religious differences, as well, most of all, my belief in a personal God, and Michal's rejection of that notion. By the time we reached the topic of the afterlife (I believe that our identities are somehow eternally continuous, and Michal opts for more of a soul-matter recycling reincarnated approach), it almost felt like there was something at stake between us in the conversation. I wanted to keep knowing her.

And, of course, we wouldn't have started dating at all had our life values not lined up so well. We both basically eschewed shopping and avoided buying whatever was new whenever possible. Our clothes were most often secondhand. She was a vegetarian and I wanted to be one. She met my kids and knew that I loved them, and we talked about what it means to raise children who are kind, giving, and inclusive. The world needs more of that. We both valued friends—just a few—and we enjoyed cooking for them, sharing a bottle of wine, and talking about more than the headlines and work. We saw each other caring for people in need.

We'd been hanging out for about nine months, and dating seriously for about two, when I asked Michal to marry me one night at her house. I was unsure of myself. It was late, my two teenagers were back at my apartment, and I was about to head home for the night to be with them. Michal and I had talked somewhat casually and hypothetically about marriage in the kitchen the day before.

"I want to talk about this marriage idea again," I began, "because yesterday I think I talked about it only in the hypothetical and so...I wanted to say...that I would like to marry you. I mean...Michal, would you marry me?" I said.

"No," she said at first. "It wouldn't work."

"Really? Why not?" I asked.

"Because. We are too different," she said, as she was thinking out loud. "Well...okay...maybe."

"Maybe?" I replied playfully.

But her maybe was a serious one. She wasn't playing.

"Yes. Maybe. I mean...how would it work? I'm not sure that it could." And this is of course part of what I love about

Michal: she's serious. We talked some more about how our religious traditions would make a relationship challenging. Michal repeated something she'd said over the past few weeks, as a rabbi who only cautiously presides at interfaith weddings, "I'm not even sure who would marry us. *I* wouldn't marry us!"

An hour later I was back in my apartment, tucking my kids into bed. Okay, you don't "tuck in" teenagers, but I made sure they were in their rooms with doors closed and begged them to eventually turn out their lights. Then, Michal phoned. I was hoping that she would.

"Yes," she softly said. "Who am I kidding: my heart says 'yes.' If we can figure it out, we can get married."

We said that we loved each other and we hung up.

I told no one for a few days. Michal left town to go to a family event in Chicago and I waited to see how she would feel about everything upon her return. I was delighted when she called from Chicago and put her father on the phone to "meet" me.

I wasn't looking forward to telling my parents, whom I called a few days later. "That seems like a big mistake," my mother said, phrasing it so as to be kind. "Jon, you need to really think about this," Dad said. A few more phone calls over the next few days and they acknowledged the reality. Later, they told me that I shouldn't have expected them to understand. Perhaps that's true, but if so, I have trouble accepting that it must be.

About a month later, Michal and I took a November weekend getaway to the coast. We were guests at the home of one of her rabbinic colleagues for Shabbat dinner and, after a warm welcome, the conversation focused on how mismatched Michal and I were, and the only way to solve the "problem" would be for me to convert to Judaism. Michal was supportive, explaining that that wasn't my intention. We both went away discouraged, not necessarily because we were doubting our ability to commit to each other, but because a seemingly like-minded colleague couldn't see how it would succeed.

In contrast, a couple of weeks after Michal and I were engaged I drove down to Massachusetts to visit an old friend, a Trappist monk, who has served as a spiritual adviser over the years. He set aside the afternoon to talk, and I told him about Michal, her Jewishness, how we connected around spiritual matters, and how much I loved her and wanted to marry her.

"And she wants to marry you?" he said.

"Yes, I think so," I responded.

"She wants to love you and live with you and be your daily companion in life?"

Again I said, "Yes, I think so."

"Well, then, that's it."

"What?"

"Let me tell you, and I feel this with my closest brothers, here: if someone wants to love me—*me*, with all of my faults and unloveableness—like that, God can only be pleased. What could possibly be wrong with that?"

MICHAL "But is it life giving?" This question seemed to become a constant throughout Jon's and my conversations. Or perhaps I remember it that way because it was a question that I loved. What could be a better lens through which to make decisions about your life, or your work, or, well, anything?

Once Jon and I were unambiguously dating, we became somewhat constant companions. We both worked from home, and I would bring my computer, and often my dog Max, over to his apartment in the afternoon to complete medical charts for the patients I had seen that morning. During the weeks Jon was without his kids he often came to me for the evenings, and eventually the nights as well.

The first formal introduction to his kids happened over homemade pizza, a Sweeney family favorite. Joe was quiet, as most fourteen-year-old boys tend to be, except perhaps when speaking into their Xbox headsets, and excused himself to his room soon after the meal. Clelia settled down with us in the living room. Jon had just acquired a thick volume of medieval poetry. I was preparing for High Holidays, for which I like to infuse the liturgy with thematic verse. After Jon and I both shared some of what was on our laps, Clelia ran upstairs and brought down a small volume, asking if she might formally "introduce" me to one of her favorite poets, Mirabai, encouraging me to take the tiny tome home with me. The evening unfolded into a delightful conversation about mystical poetry.

This scene stands in some contrast to the next family visit. One afternoon Max and I walked across the village to find Jon reading downstairs. The usual scene. But being the weekend, the kids were home, stowed away in their rooms. When a nearly six-foot-tall man suddenly showed up at the bottom of the steps, Max went into serious protection mode. While generally a sweet and friendly dog, the sixty-plus-pound Rott-weiler mix could seem rather ferocious, especially when head-ing your way at full speed and full voice. There was really no way to explain to Max that Joe lived there and did not pose a threat. It has been a tenuous relationship ever since. I mean with Joe and Max. Joe and I have figured things out over the years.

Jon is a devoted father and I loved that. I did not, however, feel comfortable with the extent to which he took care of the kids and the house. My three sisters and I were put to work when we were old enough to spread peanut butter or lift a dish without threatening its future. But as I learned more about the complicated household in which they were raised, I let go of expectations, which was good practice for when we lived in one household. But if they were *my* kids...

I shared my interest in raising a child as well as my relief at *not* bearing a child during my short previous marriage. We didn't address whether we would try to have a family should we remain together, but there was a soft sense that should a child somehow enter our lives we would embrace the gift.

According to Jewish law, our children would be Jewish. I let it be known that, were we to have children, that would be my desire as well. Jon replied with words I have heard many times since: "It would be an honor to raise a Jewish child."

Our religious lives were in flux over these months. I had finished my contract at the local synagogue and was about to begin a visiting post at a small synagogue an hour north. Jon had spent the summer preparing to convert to Catholicism, which had been drawing him for many years. His marriage was no longer an obstacle. His Episcopal priest, my friend, at whose home we first met, also lost her post that summer. So, there were no ties keeping him there.

Jon and I had not yet been to a religious service together. It had been years since I happened to visit his church and see him at the social hour. I invited him to my final service at the local synagogue and my "after party" at home, but he didn't show up, which likely contributed to my sense of our *not* being a couple and not becoming one for quite a while. I was not terribly interested in going to mass with him; he himself was struggling with the conservative nature of the local clergy and parish, and the priest was not a colleague I felt comfortable with. And of course, our being there together would have simply further complicated his conversion. He was already divorced and unwilling to go through the process of annulment. Now he would show up with me? *Oy!* Well, Father Tom would have said it differently. Jon would say he was preparing to become a "bad Catholic."

Jon did join me for some of the High Holiday services that fall. His first service was the second day of Rosh Hashanah, a morning when only a small cohort of the most dedicated and traditional members attend. The service is longer, more rigorous, and more Hebrew-laden than any other of the year. Jon loved it. His favorite moment was the silent *Amidah*, the central prayer, which is done personally before being repeated as a community. For many, this is the *least* comfortable or least rewarding section of the service. This is a man who understood, who enjoyed, prayer. Clelia joined Jon for the *Kol Nidre* service the following week. I was surprised at her appreciation for the liturgy of confession. "It feels real." And I felt that my work, my role, and my budding relationship with this family was real in a new way, too.

As a rabbi in a bucolic Vermont village, I was often contacted to officiate at weddings, usually for couples in New York or some other northeastern city looking for a "destination" wedding. Jon would enjoy hearing about the process by which I decided whether or not, and if so, how I would do these ceremonies. It was a bit of an education, and some amusement I think, to witness the gyrations of deciding for whom, and when, and why, or why not, I, or other rabbis, will officiate. He joined me for some of the events, had a keen sense of what was happening within couples and families, and quickly developed an appreciation for a good *hora*.

Jon learned enough that when he hypothetically asked how we could get married, he was pretty sure that ours was *not* a wedding I would actually officiate. And he was right, in a way. But our situation was such an outlier that it was not likely that a couple that looked like *us* would somehow show up out of the blue.

And then, a bit out of the blue, the proposal came. As an apology. In the bathtub.

"Michal, you should know, when I asked you about how we could get married, hypothetically, well, I felt bad that it was hypothetical. Because I really *do* want to marry you. Would you marry me?"

"No. I mean, who would marry us? No. Well, maybe. Well, I don't know."

Clearly I was not prepared, even as smoothly as things were moving. Jon had told me, well before we started dating, that he did *not* want to get married again. That was the safety net for all of these months. And now he had me cornered, if one can be cornered in a tub.

Jon went home, damp and disappointed. I wandered around the house, not really heading for bed. I pulled out a jar of granola and proceeded to slowly extricate each and every sunflower seed as I pondered what had just transpired. At 11 p.m. I called him.

"Well, let's see if we can figure it out. So yes, if we can figure out how to do it. So yes, maybe."

Three days later I was on a plane to Chicago for my nephew's wedding, held on Sukkot—a major Jewish holiday—which also happened to fall on a Shabbat. Meanwhile, a good friend of Jon's was moving into my house to attend Jon's conversion, which I was relieved to be missing. I didn't quite tell my family that I was sort of engaged, but I did show them Jon's picture on my phone. "Is he good in bed?" My youngest sister asked. "Yes." "Is he Jewish?" "Nope." "Figures." I am quite sure my sister has never had a relationship with a Jewish man, but I let that detail go.

My parents were pleased and unfazed by Jon's presence in my life. My dad certainly made a comment about his Irish last name and I was sure to let them know Jon was short for Jonathan, which always made me feel better. But they had ceased letting the course of my life surprise them, or perhaps just gave up trying to understand it, much like my father gave up on helping me with homework after sixth-grade geometry.

I returned to Vermont with some trepidation to find out how *we* were feeling. My trip was better than expected, his conversion was worse. And we still felt good together. And we went back to the work of figuring it out.

The most important quality in any successful romantic relationship may be—to borrow the real estate adage—commitment, commitment, commitment. Good luck getting there, however, without candor, collaboration, and compassion, for yourselves, each other, and those around you. We have yet to encounter an interfaith (or any!) couple that has survived without these qualities.

The challenges you will face may be somewhat different, but not necessarily more difficult, than those of couples more aligned on spiritual or religious issues. But presumably, those same faith factors that pose occasional difficulties are also part of what attracted you to each other. Even if your partner is quite unlike you when it comes to religious orientation or spiritual practice, there must be something about his or her perspective or practice that complements your own. Perhaps you are here trying to discover just that!

CHAPTER 6

And With This Ring

MICHAL With *this* ring I finally wed well. I had previously worn two other rings, each strangely mirroring the difficulties of the relationship it represented. Soon after becoming engaged to Jon, I stumbled upon a beautiful, old, intricate filigree band at our local village jeweler while he was out of town. He loved it, too. Having worn it for years now, I remain surprised at how little I notice it unless I deliberately stop to look, at which point I am usually stunned.

The following month, while on a weekend trip to the coast, we found a unique, embossed band for Jon, which uncannily reflected the pattern of mine. Since the process of finding his ring was quite memorable, involving poring through the stock of three large, crowded, estate jewelry stores, guided by merchants who stayed open late and opened early to accommodate us, we are slightly embarrassed that the primary association with his band remains the chocolate pecan bourbon tart we found that Sunday morning at the bakery next door. Just say "Newburyport" and watch us drool.

Jon and I married in a quick civil ceremony months before our planned spring wedding; his kids had decided they wanted to move into the house, and Jon was uncomfortable doing so without taking this step. We exchanged the rings and simply stated our intention to be married. I prepared an announcement for friends and family, which did not quite make it into the local paper:

January 2, 2010, Woodstock VT

Today, at 6:10 p.m., Michal Woll and Jon Sweeney were married in a simple civil ceremony. Friend and Windsor County Assistant Judge David Singer officiated. Also present were Jon's children, Clelia and Joseph, Michal's dog Max, and Toni Vendetti, David's wife. The bride wore a white crocheted sweater with floral appliques, floor-length blue jeans, and fuzzy blue astral-print Acorn socks. The couple exchanged antique rings. A religious ceremony and celebration is scheduled for early May.

Obviously, we eventually figured out the issues that were pending once Michal said "Yes." Long walks, late-night conversations, even discussions with close friends centered on questions such as how we would pray together, what we desired in a religious community, would we raise children, and, if so, with what traditions? And then, of course, we also needed to merge households, collaborate on finances, and sort through our stuff, of which luckily neither of us had much excess. We will discuss these things in detail in Part 3, "Creating Home."

As if this isn't enough to figure out, in the midst of all this long-term life planning, many of us choose to throw a potentially intense, expensive, and complex, yet hopefully deeply meaningful and rewarding, event. We formalize our commitment with a wedding or other ceremony and the to-do list for this can make our long-term life planning seem simple. Soon the big questions loom: Where? A church, a synagogue, a hall? By whom? A priest, a minister, imam, rabbi, friend, or some combination? And then the rest: What about attendants? And our families? The rings? Music? A color scheme? *Oy!* How are we going to do this? For some, the answer is a wedding planner. We wish there were more life planners out there to help figure out that first list.

Before we forge ahead into this rich topic, we wish to be clear that we are talking about a religious and spiritual ceremony regardless of a legal license and stand with our LGBT friends and colleagues to say it is time for full equality in marriage for everyone. There are some—including our friends Tony and Courtney—who refuse to wed before the eyes of the state until everyone is able to be married in every state. While we didn't make that choice, we are pleased that we married in a state that does have full marriage equality. We were legally married in our living room in Vermont by a local judge. But our true moment of union, our celebrated anniversary, and the majority of our joyous memories are connected to the religious ritual and spiritual gathering that happened months later—something available to everyone regardless of race, creed, gender, or sexual orientation.

Life cycle events—births, weddings, funerals—are often moments when even the proudly secular will suddenly scramble for guidance from their faith tradition. But weddings can be the most complicated. Even as the average marriage age rises, most couples marrying, at least for the first time, are young adults, the demographic group least likely to be religiously engaged. And weddings are traditionally larger, more important social events, with greater involvement of, and expectations from, parents and other family members. Even couples from the same faith background can feel unprepared to address the ritual aspects of their ceremony, which makes it all the easier to focus on the material elements of the celebration. For those distant from their tradition, without some intentional education and guidance, even having their family minister officiate a straightforward religious ceremony can leave them feeling like guests at their own wedding.

On the other hand, there are instances where children become *more* religiously engaged than the environment in which they were raised, in which case their own families can feel like strangers at the feast. Michal's family had this experience at her first wedding as well as with some of the rituals she did leading up to it.

As a rabbi in Vermont, Michal confronted yet another scenario of potential concern. Even when two Jews married each other, the vast majority of the local gathering were non-Jewish friends and colleagues who often knew little or nothing about Jewish ritual. If we are to include and engage the gathered community, we must help them understand at least a bit of what's happening.

Interfaith couples face these same issues, but with myriad added complications. You may not have thought it terribly important to marry someone who shares your faith tradition, but when it comes time to plan a ceremony it can feel essential to celebrate with your own symbols and practices.[14] If you haven't previously been particularly engaged in religious life, the sudden desire to do so may feel nothing less than jarring, especially for your partner. *What? You want to take communion? Quote First Corinthians? Read from the Qur'an? Stand under a* chuppah*? Who are you??* And while you may not have thought to do any of those things, your parents, let alone your priest or rabbi, certainly may have.

Even if you are comfortable having rituals from multiple traditions included in your ceremony, you may find that your parents will feel faint at the thought of hearing God referred to as Allah or the recitation of Hebrew or a mention of Jesus at *their* child's wedding.

Another common approach to addressing religious diversity in a wedding or commitment ceremony is creating wholly separate rituals. We have seen this most often with ethnically specific ceremonies, especially when a significant part of the family of origin still lives in another country and culture. Although we know of a number of couples that have done this, the most interesting example involved a Jewish man and Nigerian woman. The bride had converted to Judaism before the wedding. Yet over one weekend they had both a traditional Jewish wedding and a traditional Nigerian ceremony complete with festive ceremonial dress.

Spiritual elements have grown into wide use as ways of bridging faith traditions at a wedding or commitment ceremony. Unity candles are perhaps the primary example of this, new to wedding ceremonies in the last half century. Typically, two smaller taper candles are lit at the beginning of the ceremony by each partner, or by important members of each partner's family; then, by ceremony's end, each partner takes one of these lit tapers and touches it to a larger, standing pillar candle, lighting it as one flame from what previously were two—individuals, or families, or faith traditions. However, you may be surprised to discover that your local rabbi or priest does not allow their use in synagogue or church.

Sometimes it is best *not* to incorporate all religious elements into your ceremony. Our friend and Episcopal colleague Andy MacBeth writes: "I have taken part in some weddings that attempted to blend elements of both traditions, with both a rabbi and a Christian minister contributing in different ways. These were well-intentioned efforts but difficult to negotiate and ultimately not very satisfying."[15]

We have also seen it done badly. Our friends Eric and Judith, for example, married on a beautiful sunny morning in a Vermont valley with friends and family around. Eric is Baptist. Judith is Jewish. They planned what was essentially a Jewish ceremony, complete with a *chuppah* and broken glass, but it was presided over by an interfaith minister, and we couldn't help noticing the ways in which the minister was trying, unsuccessfully, to act "Jewish." After the bride walked down the aisle to the accompaniment of a Christian hymn, the minister attempted to read some Hebrew prayers, but they came out badly and some simply didn't belong in a wedding ceremony. Plus, the officiant wore a *kippah*, which seemed inappropriate or out of place for an interfaith minister, even as the sole presider over what was mostly a Jewish ceremony. We watched in disappointment—not that it was necessarily wrong, but that it was not at all what it could or should have been. Even the couple seemed to have a certain level of discomfort, which we learned later was partly a symptom of their simply not feeling well prepared.

There are success stories as well. Other couples find ways to carefully combine traditions in a ceremony. Even though they had a separate Muslim ceremony, Wendy and Ahmed included a reading of the Qur'an in their church ceremony, as well. Lainie and Phillip integrated a hand-fasting ritual and a blessing of the four winds into a simple Unitarian ceremony. Helen and David stood under a *chuppah* without any clergy, in classic Quaker style, and their *ketubah*, or wedding contract, was signed by all 127 attendees. Joan and Greg's *chuppah* stood at the center of a Buddhist *metta* meditation, invoking love and peace in concentric circles spreading like ripples into the world. Rachel and Jeremy went to great lengths to help craft their blended ceremony, carefully choosing rituals and scripture passages that, while distinctly Christian or Jewish in origin, enhanced the sense of shared sensibilities and values. Options abound, but it takes knowledge, planning, and good officiant support to make it work well.

Your family, friends, or community may be less tolerant of missteps than you expect. Not long ago, a newspaper story, a BBC radio program, and then a YouTube video offered a poignant example of this, telling the story of a group of Sikhs in early July 2012 who locked themselves in a Sikh temple in Swindon, England, eighty miles east of London, in order to disrupt plans for an interfaith marriage between a Sikh woman and a Christian man planned for that day.[16] Sikhism is known as one of the most tolerant religious faiths in the world, but when this interfaith couple planned a traditional Sikh wedding ceremony, called the *Anand Karaj*, it was too much for the protestors to accept. They took what most people would agree was an inappropriate step to voice their concern, but the couple, or the clergy, may also have been at fault; they may have shown a lack of sensitivity. Ultimately, the couple married in a civil ceremony.

There are so many variables and so many people to consider. In many ways, the participants in a wedding ceremony consist of concentric circles, with the couple in the middle, surrounded by family, clergy, dear friends, and then the broader community. You want the ceremony to reflect your true selves while keeping the other circles in mind. In this chapter, you will see moments when Michal clearly addressed the needs of a couple's parents. But she has also been known to say, "Your *mother* is not the one getting married!" and then offer to take the heat for decisions that were important and appropriate for the couple, and potentially difficult for the family. The challenge to create the perfect ceremony is maximizing the depth of meaning without wholly sacrificing personal comfort for you, and for those important to you.

MICHAL "You *would* perform an interfaith wedding?" My mother was surprised. She saw me as someone "very religious"

and knew that within her synagogue milieu, which was decidedly less traditional in practice but chock-full of parents with non-Jewish in-laws, an interfaith wedding wouldn't happen.

"It depends on the couple, of course. But it seems rather hypocritical to warmly welcome, even recruit, interfaith families as paying members of your *shul* after you've rejected the opportunity to help them create the family in the first place." This position seemed to appear organically within me; it wasn't a product of my training. Even as a "young" rabbi (I am in the sixth year of my rabbinic career but am decidedly middle-aged), I spent well over a decade fine-tuning my approach to interfaith marriage, having performed my first wedding early in seminary.

I recall a conversation I had with my first bride, in a loud whisper while leaning awkwardly over the circulation counter in the seminary library. She came from a conservative Jewish family and had done a lot of personal work around her own surprise at marrying a Catholic man. It was in the middle of the day between classes, but there was some urgency for her around one final decision:

"I understand, it *is* a lot of Hebrew for his family. But if the traditional seven blessings aren't included, it won't feel like a real Jewish wedding to *yours*."

Her fiancé was equally uneasy at the beginning; at our first meeting he made little eye contact. The process of creating their ceremony was difficult for them and complicated for me to guide them through. After many meetings I asked the couple to throw out all the tidbits of ideas for readings and other elements they had collected and to shift their focus. I asked, "Who are you as a couple and as individuals? What do you wish your gathered loved ones to know about you and your union?"

Ultimately they had a lovely wedding, under a *chuppah* made from an Italian lace tablecloth from the groom's great-grandmother's trousseau. Yes, they included the Hebrew blessings, but also English interpretations read by the groom's family, a long lineup of young, freckled, Catholic attendants, and special elements created specifically for and with this couple—silent vows exchanged in silk pouches, a sledge-hammer painted white and adorned with a silver bow, used by each of them to smash a goblet. It was a wonderful event, and for many years afterward I remained friends with the couple and became the family rabbi—primarily for the extended Catholic family.

Determining which weddings to officiate has been a process of trial and error for me. I thought I was doing a good job of figuring out which couples were committed to a Jewish family life, who were willing to personally invest in the process of creating a ceremony and were more concerned about the meaning of their wedding than the shade of red in the tablecloths.

And so I still shudder when I think of what has affectionately come to be called the "Connecticut Wedding from Hell," one of the "destination" weddings I officiated in Vermont. Held at a spa and resort in the far southwest corner of the state, this interfaith wedding was an overwhelmingly superficial experience. Had I been too subtle in explaining the conflict between Jewish tradition and the diamond wedding band? Had I spent too long negotiating over just how early I would start on a Saturday evening, before Shabbat was over?

It was like Abraham negotiating for the people of Sodom: what if we started at 6:45? But why not 6:30? Well, in *that* case...I suggest that couples *not* tell clergy that if they don't start early enough on Shabbat afternoon they won't be able to take full advantage of the open bar that evening.

Once at the venue, I felt like I was being handled on a movie set by too many "best boys." The bride and her entourage were endlessly whining about their dresses and hair. All the men, Jews included, looked uncomfortable balancing the provided yarmulkes on their slicked-back hair, especially after the ceremony while trying to drop their shrimp cocktails into their mouths without staining their tuxes. It was hard to gather the focus and energy of the couple and other participants or create space for meaning or reflection.

Of course, the difficulties I had with this particular event could just have easily occurred with a wedding between two Jews, including the detail of timing that seems to be the issue currently stressing many of my colleagues. This matter reached the public eye in the firestorm following Chelsea Clinton's wedding, co-officiated by a rabbi and minister on a Shabbat afternoon.

On the other hand, there was the wedding that I didn't officiate, which also touched me deeply. Sharon and Ian were a Jewish woman and an Irish—yes, as in from Ireland—Catholic. They came to me for advice about integrating Jewish tradition into their wedding, which would be officiated on a Saturday afternoon by a personal friend of the bride's, who was a Catholic priest. During our first meeting Sharon began to cry. "I always dreamed that when I married we would stand under a *chuppah*, step on a glass, and everyone would yell '*mazal tov!*' "

She was not my first bride to wrestle with conflict between the love she found and the life she had imagined.

At our subsequent discussions we reviewed the structural aspects of a Jewish wedding, the traditional series of blessings, opportunities for both families to comfortably participate. The couple had decided *not* to incorporate any aspects of the Catholic mass and to also leave out the *Kiddush*, the traditional blessing over wine, so as not to give the appearance of performing a sacrament. I explained that this was in line with a classic Talmudic concept of *marit ayin*, meaning "the appearance of the eye." One shouldn't do something appropriate if it could *look* inappropriate and therefore lead to confusion.

A couple of weeks before the wedding, I got a slightly frantic call from Sharon. They hadn't realized that their British priest could not sign the legal license and they were wondering if I would do that for them. After wrestling with the details of the situation for a few moments, I decided to attend the wedding primarily as an observer and sign the license for them later that day. Upon my arrival, I was introduced to a delightful young man, Father Tom, who inquired how to properly pronounce the word "*chuppah*," which he would be explaining to the gathering. I taught him to use a perfect Israeli accent, and he said it well.

Father Tom conducted an ecumenical, spiritual, Jewishly structured wedding and explained the symbolism of the rings and the *chuppah*, which draped above them. As the ceremony concluded, Father Tom told us all about the glass in his hand, how breaking it would symbolize the breaking of barriers between people, and requested that after it was broken everyone yell "*mazal tov!*" As the recessional played, the woman seated next to me, whom I'd gotten to know a bit before the ceremony began, leaned over and whispered, "Such a shame he is a priest. He is adorable! You two would be such a good match!" I managed a wry smile and softly sighed. "It's always something."

After the crowd around Sharon subsided, I found her and said, "You go girl! You knew what you wanted and you made it happen. That was beautiful."

I am still quite sure this was a wedding that, if asked, I would not have officiated, even if it was not held on Shabbat afternoon. Sharon and Ian planned to create a home and raise children with multiple faith traditions. But it perfectly represented the vision I have shared with other couples who wished to have an interfaith ceremony that I could not perform: Find someone you like and trust to do the ceremony—a minister or judge or friend who can get a license for a day. Research your traditions. Discover what will be meaningful for you and important for you and your families. Involve the people in your lives who are knowledgeable and helpful, and have *your* best interest at heart. Let me know how I can be helpful.

Not all clergy are willing or able, according to the rules of their denominations or affiliations, to perform an interfaith ceremony. The Catholic Church, for example, has been famously stringent on this front, one symptom being the documents couples need to sign regarding their commitment for living a Catholic life and raising Catholic children. Over recent decades, however, even these documents have become more intentional and less prescriptive. Jewish clergy are also historically less open to performing interfaith weddings than their Protestant counterparts, although within all the religious traditions there is great variation between and within denominations, as well as a gradual shift toward more support of the practice.

Requesting that clergy co-officiate a ceremony in tandem with a colleague from a different tradition will further narrow the pool of potential participants. So, if your first choice of clergy says that she or he cannot perform your ceremony, don't be too surprised. Hopefully that person or someone else can refer you to someone who can. But we suggest you go about this thoughtfully. A lowest common denominator factor is sometimes at work here, because the clergyperson who is willing to do just about anything to make you happy is not necessarily the best one for your ceremony or the best one to make your day meaningful.

Of course, in the 21st century there is one way of finding *anything*—the Internet. And, as you would imagine, there are countless sites advertising wedding officiants, many of whom promise to do whatever type of ceremony you wish. There are numerous websites for "interfaith rabbis," which is a term that doesn't exist outside of the wedding industry. We have no doubt that many of these individuals will do a wonderful job with your wedding, but we don't know how to determine which ones they might be. So, count on personal referrals from friends and local clergy. If you are interested in finding a rabbi who has been vetted, however, there is a website particularly aimed at interfaith couples where you can go for referrals: InterfaithFamily.com. This site is designed specifically for couples with one Jewish partner. No other religious group or denomination has yet to, or perhaps needed to, create a similar resource online.

Again our friend and Episcopal priest Andy MacBeth offers great advice that echoes Michal's own approach: "One option for interfaith couples is to be married in a civil ceremony by a friendly judge or wedding commissioner, while inviting the families' spiritual leaders each to participate by offering a prayer—or simply being guests." Civil ceremonies and religious ceremonies are different animals, and sometimes a civil ceremony is the simplest answer.

There is also the possibility that you do not want anyone to "perform" or "preside over" your ceremony, because you would rather do it yourself. This is becoming more common. It also is a choice that makes sense in certain traditions (Quakers, Islam, and Judaism, in particular), where there have long been traditions of couples marrying each other before family and friends, rather than anyone else "marrying them." An officiant is needed only to sign the legal license. This is what we did. More on that below.

And so the journey begins, as you try to get from the "I will" (marry you) to the "I do." A successful one will involve a lot of soul searching, discernment, communication, and honesty. Ideally, the process of getting married will help you chart the course of your marriage and your family life together. It is too easy to begin this process by focusing on your rings or a dress, or the messages you are already getting from your family, or the expectations of your social group. We suggest you stop right there and refocus on each other and your visions, shared and individual, for the many decades of life ahead of you. Consider your priorities and values. This may be the time you discover much more about this event than the religious content. If one of you wants to be married on a cruise ship in the Bahamas and the other wants the ceremony to take place in a cabin in the woods, there may be broader issues to discuss.

You can easily spend a lot of money. Between rings, dresses, tuxes, food, booze, flowers, rented halls and tents and tables and chairs, and a band, tens of thousands of dollars can quickly slip away. You'll find that, as you think carefully about your ceremony, almost nothing is value-neutral. What you may want most of all is to create a beautiful ceremony, one that represents you and the life you are beginning together.

JON Everyone in the office kept telling me to look out for moose. "They're everywhere up there!" someone warned. "Be careful, especially since you're driving at night," added another. Within two weeks of moving to Vermont, I was headed to the Northeast Kingdom in the upper portion of the state. "Will absolutely *crush* your car. And *you*, if you're not careful!" someone chimed in as I left the office for the weekend.

"I get it. Okay, I'll drive carefully," I replied. The fresh, flatlander, goyish marketing vice president of a Jewish publishing house, I had little firsthand experience with Jewish ritual, and the Conference on Judaism in Rural New England was having its biannual meetings in late October in St. Johnsbury, Vermont. I would drive up on Saturday in time for *havdalah*. I also had little experience with Vermont at that point, but my colleagues must have been either messing with me or paranoid about moose. I remained in Vermont for fifteen years and saw only two moose in all my time on thousands of miles of back roads.

But I vividly remember that first *havdalah*, a service to mark the end of Shabbat. I remember the beautiful darkness of the Vermont sky and how illumined it was by the lighting of the *havdalah* candle—a special, braided candle with multiple wicks—as well as prayers that were said in both Hebrew and English. Then, blessings were said over small bundles of spices that were passed around from person to person. Each one raised them to his nose and took the aroma in with deep appreciation. No one told me what to do, but I watched those beside me and tried to do likewise. A blessing was said over the wine and it was drunk. The *havdalah* candle was extinguished with a hiss in a small saucer containing some of the wine, and Shabbat was over. People sang and danced. Those rural New England Jews could dance! At that point I mostly watched, but was moved by it all.

I learned that *havdalah* is intended to require us to use all five senses. We can't help feeling involved in it. We see the flame of the candle; we taste the wine; we smell the spices; we feel the candle's heat; and we hear the prayers, blessings, and song. Little did I know then, in 1997, that I would marry a rabbi thirteen years later, with *havdalah* as the backbone of our ceremony!

Michal and I married first in a civil ceremony, standing in the living room before a friend who was a local judge. It took almost no planning beyond the meal we served to our guests afterward. We exchanged rings, asking each other to wear them as a symbol of our commitment. My two children, ages fifteen and seventeen, were there. It took a total of six minutes.

Then, Michal and I began to prepare our religious ceremony, to be held later that spring on a Vermont hillside. I wanted something simple and religiously appropriate, and I didn't want to feel foolish performing rituals that were too foreign to me. I remember saying early on, "Let's not have a lot of Hebrew." And, "Please, let's explain everything, step by step. Let's walk through it—in order to see if it is comfortable."

I had no hope—or frankly, need—to marry in the Church. Like Michal, who felt she'd already had the "perfect" Jewish wedding once before, I had already had a complete Christian wedding. Now, I was happy to do something different.

Also, as a new Catholic, I knew that I *wouldn't* be married in the Church. For months my priest had encouraged me to pursue an annulment of my first marriage. I resisted in part because I didn't think I ever wanted to marry again, and because any argument for annulling my first marriage seemed like a gargantuan stretch. I realize, now, that I probably could have obtained one, but it doesn't at all matter, as Michal and I still wouldn't have wanted to marry in the Church.

My family had no experience with Jewish ritual before coming to our wedding, and I wanted them to feel comfortable. Things had started out somewhat uneasy between Michal and my parents, but once they spent time with her, they came to love and appreciate her. What started tenuously with my announcement one day on the phone that I'd asked a Jewish woman they'd never met to marry me became a classic case of how familiarity overcomes otherness. "She is wonderful," my mother said to me at Thanksgiving, a day after meeting Michal face-to-face for the first time. "I can see why you love her." She paused, then added: "I approve."

So I was pleased when my parents then agreed to come up from Florida for our ceremony in early May. It was important to us to incorporate my Christian family into our service in a way that would be ritually appropriate, and yet comfortable for them and easy to understand.

My kids had gotten to know Michal even before we started dating, but the adjustment to Dad marrying someone other than their mother is still a tough one, no matter how resilient and mature the kids may be. Also, Judaism was entirely new to them, and they were both at a place in life where they had little appreciation for either religion or ritual. We wanted the kids included, too, but again, only in ways that would be both ritually appropriate and comfortable.

I think that we found those balances, and thankfully, Michal drove the process. Her gift is for creating meaningful ritual. I knew as much from a year's worth of praying together, as well as watching her officiate at religious services, weddings, and bar/bat mitzvahs. Starting with *havdalah*, for instance, was Michal's idea—but it was one that immediately resonated with me.

My beautiful, seventeen-year-old daughter, Clelia, held the *havdalah* candle. On a starry Vermont evening with friends gathered around, she began the service, holding the giant candle while it was lit. Then she lifted it high in the air. Her face shined in its glow. Each of our seventy friends was holding a small, individual candle, and these were all lit, one-by-one, starting with the *havdalah* candle. Once the whole hillside was full of stands of light, we all touched them to a waiting pile of brush, sticks, and logs, creating a roaring bonfire. The symbolism was intentional! The day was May 1 on the secular calendar; but more importantly it was *Lag B'Omer*, a festive day on the Hebrew calendar, when Jews mark the end of a period of mourning (remembering thousands who died in a medieval plague), by celebrating in a variety of ways—including getting married. And bonfires.

We also had a circling ritual, revaluing the traditional Jewish tradition of having the bride circle the groom seven times. First, Michal circled me. Then I circled her. And then our families circled around us and eventually everyone else circled around them, all symbolizing their support for this new thing we were creating. There was Spirit, or *Ruach*, on that hillside! And that's what we wanted most of all.

Friends often ask me, kindly and tentatively, "Have you given up a lot in marrying Michal?" In other words, don't I miss being somehow more Christian? Didn't I miss marrying in a church? I answer: no, I really haven't, and no, I didn't. Our wedding ceremony was rich in a way that standing together in church would not have been. I have always appreciated complexity in life, as well as change, and my relationship with Michal, as well as our wedding celebration, was made more beautiful by the symbols, spirit, and intention that went into them, and the differences between us that came together, too.

What an honor it was for me to be able to experience and plan it together with the woman I love.

One other important process worth mentioning for me, in preparing our wedding ceremony, is how Michal and I imagined our vows. This is of course important for every couple, but as one who'd previously vowed to a woman "till death do us part," it was poignant.

Michal and I discussed our previous marriages all over again in the context of planning our ceremony. I told her again how my first marriage had ended: unhappy though it was, not until my wife left me. I wouldn't have ever left her. My vows and my evangelical conscience made that option unimaginable. Then came the critical moment. Michal looked at me and said, "Don't ever think that you're doing me or the world a favor by staying in an unhappy marriage. I want you to leave if that is ever the case!" What a hero I thought I'd been all those years for staying with my ex-wife and disavowing my own desires. That clearly wouldn't be the case married to Michal.

After that, our vows to each other became clear. We would not vow to love and cherish, et cetera, until death do us part. We left that out. There was a profound, although silent, intention behind the vows that we spoke out loud at our ceremony, and it is this: As long as our marriage is good for the two of us, and good for the world, it is what my evangelical forebears would call "God's will." If it ever becomes something other than that, we will know, and dissolution is negotiable—and acceptable.

In both Judaism and Islam, marriage is traditionally understood as a kind of social contract. By writing a *ketubah* or *katb el-kitab* (they are the same word, one is Hebrew, the other Arabic), they make promises to each other, and if these are ever broken, someone has cause for divorce. From the beginning, they recognize that marriages can fall apart for a variety of reasons. From the start, they don't assume that any union is "made in heaven" or "till death do us part." My first marriage was of the supposed "made in heaven" variety, which meant that its dissolution caused a whole host of problems and consternations. I'm talking about a lot more than feelings of failure. Guilt and more guilt. God was "watching" and shaking his mighty finger at me. This is why the vows that Michal and I said to each other at our wedding were a radical departure for me. I spent months explaining the absence of "till death do us part" to friends and family before and afterward, and interestingly, to a person, including those who remain within the religious milieu of my childhood, they understood.

MICHAL When Jon and I decided to wed, we easily found a date and chose a venue. Whether the ground would be dry enough on May 1 to park cars on our friend's farm or we would all need to wear boots to reach the hilltop were variables we were willing to let unfold. We were thrilled that a minor Jewish holiday, traditionally marked by bonfires and weddings, would occur that year on a Saturday evening. That it was also May Day and International Worker Solidarity Day further sweetened the pot. We chose a format that most of my couples tend to reject—hosting a celebratory meal followed by the ceremony after sundown.

But the ceremony was a challenge. We knew we would not ask any of our many clergy friends to be the formal "officiant" for a variety of reasons, primarily the fact that I would be breaching my own rabbinic boundaries. So we planned to have our friend and local judge be present and do the legal honors. That need evaporated when we essentially eloped months earlier.

Based on our plans for family, home, and religious life together, Jon and I seemingly needed the same type of ceremony that I create for all my couples, built on the classic Jewish framework and personalized from there. But each time we began to plan, it was clear to me this wasn't going to be right for our wedding. As I imagined being on that hilltop together there was never a *chuppah* over our heads. On a visceral level, it felt too confining—I wanted a canopy of stars. Perhaps that was the symbol for the ceremony writ large—it was too narrow for our spiritual and religious lives.

When I work with couples, many of whom have little or no active or intellectual connection to Jewish life, I find creating the ceremony allows them to engage with or renew this aspect of their lives and their knowledge. The traditions and symbols are also tools to help them embrace the religious path they have chosen and/or are affirming. Jon and I didn't have that need; our religious knowledge and experience was rich and deep. But forcing our religious lives into a classic Jewish ceremony felt false. I was clear about a future that did not include having Jon convert, and equally clear that we would only have a *chuppah* and *ketubah*, a wedding contract, when that day (never) happened. And I know that somewhere within me was the memory of having already done all that, in detail, all the way down to personally hand writing and painting our *ketubah*. Now I wanted something different, something more.

Since we were marrying on Saturday night we began with the *havdalah* ceremony, performed at the end of Shabbat and representing the separation between the holy day and the rest of the week, and then gleaned elements from both the *havdalah* and wedding liturgies. Fire from the twisted *havdalah* candle was transferred to scores of candles held by each guest. Eventually these flames merged into a huge bonfire. The tradition of having a bride circle the groom, now often done in a more egalitarian manner by progressive couples, rippled out from our circling each other, to circling together, inviting our families to join us, and finally having everyone there create a huge spiral of flame and song around us. The glass of wine was passed from hand to hand as each guest added their own blessing for us.

We made vows to each other, taking turns making promises, only one of which we had scripted together. Jon did not quite render that written vow *in toto*; he forgot a line. To this day I still remind him at appropriate moments that he did *not* promise to be honest to me. We haven't yet determined the statute of limitations on this point.

I loved our ceremony! It was ritually complex and meaningful. It allowed many of our clergy friends to use their skills and all of our loved ones to participate. Most thought it was quite traditional and very Jewish, while it was actually quite radical Jewishly. And we successfully incorporated our parents and Jon's children into a scenario that could have been uncomfortable all around. Even Max got into the mix—showing up at our feet, wrapped in a celebratory bandanna, just as we began to speak to each other.

Where your mixed-up relationship is headed is something only you can know. Every process of getting to know each other can feel a bit like driving a switchback road in the mountains. As you travel it the first time, you feel every turn, often uneasily in your stomach, especially if you've taken it quickly. You reach a stopping point, perhaps in hope of a "scenic view," and look to the road just ahead, yet all you can usually glimpse are the next turn or two. The others are lost in the trees or around a corner.

Most of us travel such a road over and over again. We can spend decades trying to find someone we can't live without, and the stomach queasies come and go with the territory of every relationship. You don't have to wrestle with faith in order to experience all of that. But if we take this road thoughtfully, asking the right questions, listening well, differences between faiths (or none) can become an opportunity for an uncommonly scenic ride.

PART III

Creating Home

Our homes are sanctuaries, meant to reflect our needs, our desires, our priorities. And *home* need not refer only to the place where we sleep at night. It's also where our families and communities gather. A mosque, synagogue, or zendo can also be home. As our world gets simultaneously bigger and smaller, more connected and more isolated, and certainly more complex, it seems that home, in all of its dimensions, is more important than ever. Whether you are committed or wed, or simply making a home together, you will want to create a place that is a sanctuary for your values, interests, and spirit. You may also decide together to seek a home within a religious community. You may desire to pray, together or individually. And perhaps eventually, all or some of this will be passed along to your children. "Home is where the heart is," you might say. "If we can find love together, we can create a home and a family." We believe that is true. We also know that too often not enough thought and care are put into sorting out the details around these issues before the cake is cut. So we invite you to take some time to consider your future religious lives together.

———

CHAPTER 7

Our December Dilemma

We begin this important part of our book in the place where most interfaith discussions seem to climax: What to do come December when the holidays are approaching? Every year, the media is full of stories about this. Only in December, apparently, is there something relevant and tangible about interfaith religion in the home because there's a sense that conflict is brewing, or inevitable. Or at least, that's what the media tells us. But it can indeed be challenging to address the demands of competing faith traditions, especially when the broader culture suggests that December is the only time that faith enters into our lives.

Our take on the so-called December dilemma is different from others'. We begin this section about "Home" right here, not because navigating the holidays is the most important topic. On the contrary, we'd like to address this "dilemma" in order to move on to the bulk of our religious lives.

When Thanksgiving rolls by, we face certain problems,

but *not* because the upcoming season is the only time when religious symbols and celebrations are near the center of our lives. Instead, we face a couple of other dilemmas. First, how do we disengage from the prevailing culture of materialism and excess that characterizes this season? Second, how do we thoughtfully engage with our extended families, who may be celebrating a different holiday? And yes, sometimes these two dilemmas end up juxtaposed with each other, which can create the most awkward scenario of all.

To the first dilemma, Black Friday has darkened the whole enterprise of the December holidays. In our home, we struggle not to have our passion for faith zapped before Thanksgiving ever arrives. For example, it used to be Jon's favorite day of the year, a time to get together with beloved family rarely seen, and Jon's family had a knack for doing it well: eating well, football in the backyard, celebrating life, and toasting God with gratitude. These days it is hard to finish your pumpkin pie before the gift buying begins, as some stores don't even close for that one day, or re-open before the coffee turns cold. At the Thanksgiving table, now, we often find ourselves surrounded by conversations about which stores people plan to hit and in what order, as soon as dinner is over.

It can easily feel like consumerism has become the real December religion, regardless of your tradition of origin. We spend and spend, and if we don't, we are accused by family or friends or colleagues of being scrooges or somehow unhappy. Madison Avenue knows our brains better than we do ourselves. The advertising industry has convinced us to chase after shadows of the ideal home, the ideal family, in ways that cause us to believe we can create happiness—or at least warm feelings—with food and stuff, which seem to be the primary elements of what every perfect holiday looks like. There is so much pressure in December—on memory, on time, on finances—pressure that stresses many relationships, regardless of how in-line your at-home religious affiliation may be.

The recent merging of Hanukkah and Christmas may have been the first symptom of this trend. In his recent book, *A Kosher Christmas: 'Tis the Season to Be Jewish*, Joshua Plaut describes in detail the focused efforts of the Jewish community over the last century to transform Hanukkah from a minor holiday to a major celebration that could successfully compete with Christmas.[17] It was once the case that Jewish children learned otherwise at home in December, whereas now celebrating Christmas and celebrating Hanukkah have become pretty much the same thing. One can have trouble distinguishing them except for the symbols: the garland in Jewish homes might have sparkling little Stars of David on it.

Yet in other ways Christmas and Hanukkah were already the same. The timing of both holidays most likely evolved as repackaging of ancient pagan solstice festivals, celebrating the shift from a world hurtling into darkness to a world once again becoming light. There is no question from a textual standpoint that Jesus was not born in the wintertime; shepherds don't tend flocks in Bethlehem in December. And the actual meaning of the Hebrew word "*hanukkah*" is dedication, referring to the rededication of the temple in Jerusalem many years after it was defiled and inhabited by the

Romans. The rabbis of the Talmudic period created the tale of the miracle of the oil in the temple to divert the focus of the holiday from a tale of war, which it mostly was.

Of course, materialism is not only an American problem, or a Western problem, or a problem of first-world nations. The globalizing reach of advertising's ability to stimulate the Pavlovian dogs of our desire is almost never-ending. The *New York Times* reported recently that even Buddhist monks in Thailand were saddened to realize how their ancient religious practices are fast becoming irrelevant, when they used to be regarded as central. Temples that used to be closely intertwined with village life are now almost vacated and absent of monks. "Consumerism is now the Thai religion," they reported, quoting one of the country's most respected monks. "In the past, people went to temple on every holy day. Now, they go to shopping malls."[18] This is happening everywhere, and it is noticeable before every holiday; aisles of stuff presented as essentials for proper celebration. We can't help thinking that Madison Avenue has won, making us all into consumers, first and foremost.

Even belief in Santa Claus is worth a little (okay, maybe a lot of) criticism. The earnestness with which so many parents, even schools, civic groups, the postal service, and communities of all sorts push childhood belief in Santa's existence only makes sense in a world that is post-Christian, in the sense that the big guy has filled the vacuum created by the loss of religious beliefs. Santa is the new faith for the secular life and therefore has been deemed appropriate for school hallways and winter concerts.

Nathan Englander's short story "Reb Kringle," about a

rabbi who for decades dons a Santa outfit in December to work at a downtown New York City department store and earn extra cash, shines a hilarious light on all of this.[19] The action begins in the sanctuary of the synagogue, where we meet this *rebbe*. His wife is badgering him to get to work on time at the department store—because doing Santa one month a year helps to pay the mortgage for both the *shul* and the roof over their heads. He's less enthusiastic than she is about this job of his.

"It's a sin..." he tells his wife. "It's not," she responds: "Where does it say that playing with *goyishe* children is a sin?" Reb Kringle says, "Playing!...Anyone who has seen it would never call such mayhem playing. Not since the time of Noah has the world seen such boundless greed." The story concludes with the *rebbe*, as Santa, hearing a Jewish child make a confession while sitting on his lap: his new Christian stepfather won't allow him to celebrate Hanukkah anymore. "Church and no Hanukkah!" he yells, ranting, screaming, looking for the mother, hilariously and furiously quitting on the spot, even as he reminds the store management that with his natural flowing white beard and bellowing belly, he's a much more real Santa than any of their other hired icons. But Reb Kringle's conscience is finally pricked when the holiday that pays him so well gets in the way of one boy's religious observance.

We realize that not everyone is Jewish and Christian, and that differences in Christmas expectations can turn even a couple comprised of two Christians into an intermarriage of sorts. One's tradition of midnight mass and simple stockings may seem as foreign as Timbuktu to another interested in caroling door-to-door and mountains of boxes under the tree. Couples with other religious backgrounds, too, as well as devoutly anti-religious atheists, must find their way of inhabiting this culture overwhelmed with material Christmas.

One young Muslim, Huma Qureshi,[20] explains how her family navigates life in a Christian world, including an upbringing in Christian parochial schools, and experiences with her Christian in-laws. Her Muslim family celebrated Christmas throughout her childhood, as of course many families of other faiths, and none, do. The celebration "was (and is) about being on holiday and getting together with friends and family, something festive and bright to cheer up the winter drear," she explains, and then continues: "I imagine this is how it is for most people." Qureshi was surprised to discover years later that, other than the addition of trees and presents, Christmas with her husband's extended Christian family felt very much the same.

Qureshi's story is a perfect segue to the issue of engaging with our extended families, even though her own home is not an interfaith one—her husband converted to Islam before they wed. The potential challenge they face in honoring her husband's family of origin and sharing important family events is not very different from that faced by interfaith couples. Sensitivity is key. And you may face occasions when you are forced to choose between upholding your values versus making family happy.

The process by which you might navigate holidays, celebrations, and festivals is not so different from all the other decisions you have faced with your partner. It takes communication and clarity, only now your family is a participant in the process as well. You will want to find ways to help your partner understand how to include your family in a way that is comfortable for you and vise versa. This may involve requesting limits on gifting or stressing sensitivity around the religious language used about their beliefs. Strive to explore your ability to be flexible and understanding. Extended family celebrations can actually be a wonderful way to expose children to the faith or background of a parent and allow them to enjoy a holiday that they don't celebrate at home, thus not confusing the identity, or at least intention, you have chosen for your family. Of course, this only works if it occurs within a value set that feels appropriate, or at least tolerable, for you.

The real religious minority at this time of year may have shifted over the decades from the non-Christians forced to endure public Christianity through calendar, symbol, and song to those, Christian or Muslim or Sikh or whatever, who are religiously and spiritually engaged. There are those of us who want to rethink this whole time of year, to not just bring it back to sanity, but to reimagine our celebrations almost completely.

For Jews, this can mean simplifying Hanukkah once again, returning it to the observance of a miracle that it once was, complete with games and *gelt*, but without the Christmas trappings. Some in the Jewish community, for instance, have long made it a habit of serving or delivering Christmas meals to those in need, or working in hospitals, public safety departments, and other settings that never close in order to let their Christian colleagues or other coworkers who wish to have a holiday.

For Christians, this rethinking can mean rediscovering the meaning of the season by focusing on the themes of Advent. Lasting for four weeks between Thanksgiving and Christmas Day, Advent is about counting the days and reflecting as we wait for God in our lives, as we look for God who wants always to be among us. This is an opportunity to renew our commitments to faith, giving, and kindness, represented by the light of that star that represented God's presence in the millennia-old story. Some Christians are also beginning to rediscover the real, historical Saint Nicholas. Nicholas of Myra was a fourth-century Greek-speaking bishop who lived in what is today Turkey. He actually *did* go around distributing gifts to needy children, finding kids in desperate need, often giving secretly so as not to be noticed, perhaps even—yes it is true—by dropping gifts down family chimneys!

All these aspects of the tradition lead to the good work that *does* occur more often at this time of year. If we acknowledge that God is among us, we must feed those who are hungry and care for those in need. St. Nick is a reminder to give to that child who has little, not an excuse to obtain the latest gadget. So, for families that want to revalue Christmas along these lines, Christmas morning may still involve gifts, but the celebration of what is received might be more in balance with what the kids have learned to give. These are ways to curb the excesses and focus on more important aspects of the meaning of God in our lives. We would like to see these celebrations of religious traditions stand in the way of the secular religious freight train more meaningfully and more often.

There's no conflict in our house around the holidays because neither of us is interested in racing around to buy stuff, and we both appreciate meaningful religious ritual. While we brought somewhat different personal experiences and concerns around these holidays to our relationship, we quickly found that we were kindred souls as we spent our first fall together as a couple.

"Wouldn't it be great if, instead of buying stuff the day after Thanksgiving, we all went through our closets and gave some stuff away to people who need it more than us?" we pondered that first year. Then, after a friend dubbed it "Thanksgive-away," the spiritual practice quickly become an annual tradition for us and others. It started that first year as a Facebook conversation, followed the next with a rallying cry on the *Huffington Post*'s religion page, and today it may be our favorite winter holiday! Perhaps if Thanksgiveaway became part of a serious cultural observance, the December news reports would no longer bother reporting aggregate spending as a barometer of "consumer confidence," but rather, broadcast indications of generosity as a gauge of our human spirit.

JON I love December. Always have. Unlike many of my friends, I actually enjoy the days becoming darker and darker. The end of the year brings out the contemplative in me. Since time began there have been dangers associated with the darkness, first from whatever was lurking outside, and then from whatever we might discover inside of us; but as Isaiah says, salvation comes with the dawn. That is our hope and expectation.

I love this aspect of Christmas, too, how it values anticipation and silence, as we wait for God to come among us. Those Christians of old who decided to celebrate Christmas near the winter solstice, in my opinion, really knew what they were doing. If only we felt all the time the way that we sometimes feel on a late December evening.

But my relationship with Christmas is also complicated. Even though I was an earnest young evangelical believer in my parents' home, when Christmas came around each year I experienced it entirely around presents. I don't think that was my parents' fault—we certainly went to church all the time, and they taught me otherwise—maybe it's just kid-nature. I remember the situation getting so bad one December, when I was about twelve, that I stayed home "sick" from school in order to rummage through my father's dresser and find receipts for gifts already wrapped, so I could look them up in the J. C. Penney catalog.

After I became a parent, I took my two older kids to church all through Advent and talked at home about what the "real" Christmas meant. But primary conversations in our household during the season still revolved too much around what to get the kids for Christmas, and the kids were just as focused on what they were getting as I had been. As they grew into teenagers, I was grateful to begin pulling us—or at least, myself—slowly out of that cyclone.

A change in my approach to the season was beginning to happen when Michal and I met. I'd lost interest in Christmas trees a year or two earlier when I moved from the property in Vermont. There we had a family ritual of finding and cutting down our tree on the hill behind our house while intoning a beautiful prayer that my daughter composed, thanking the earth for it. Still, once cut and dressed, those trees mostly became canopies for wrapped gifts. I was slowly putting away the other accoutrements of Christmas, too.

One of the many benefits of marrying Michal was that, since we decided to make Judaism the faith at home, I had a good reason to jettison secular Christmas. It has turned out to be a blessing. I think it is nearly impossible for Christmas gift-giving to shape our lives for good. Perhaps thank-you notes and small checks for the mail delivery person, that sort of thing, but not the industry of shopping, buying, wrapping, grumbling, and coveting. Today, I try to thoughtfully select one present for each of my kids, and tell them how much I love them. Other gifts go to charities that we discuss together. Then, I send a monastery fruitcake to my parents, and to my brother and his family, but that's really about it. Those are all gifts that I feel good about.

So, at the risk of sounding like Linus to Charlie Brown, let me say what Christmas is about for me, now. I love midnight mass. It is beautiful. I love the candles, the contemplation, and the music—reverent, solemn, and familiar. It reminds me of the quiet intoning of prayer that happens in a monastery in the early hours of the morning. I don't much mind the absence of young children at such services, because although children's choirs and pageants are fun for parents at Christmastime, they are not as important for those who simply want to worship. I prefer midnight mass in the same way that I prefer daily, early-morning mass rather than Saturday nights or Sunday mornings. More quiet and reverence, an opportunity to stop, think, and pray.

The original Christmas was of course without fanfare; it was the birth of Jesus, pure and simple. The story is beautiful, and I think that the essential meaning of this season is a reminder that God wants to be with us. *Immanuel.* God wants to be close to me, and for me to be close to him. I need to continually try to make room for God in my life. As the medieval Dominican mystic Meister Eckhart once said in a Christmas sermon, "If the birth of God doesn't happen in me, what good is it?" Which basically means, how will it shape my life?

I like to focus on renewing my religious life and moral commitments this time of year. I go to mass in December, and pray for the birth of God in a new way in my life, but I also look around and wish that the inside of the church wasn't all dolled up.

MICHAL Growing up, Christmas day was celebrated as it was by many Jewish families in metropolitan areas: a movie and Chinese food. It felt like a real tradition and it worked. As a child, my family would often head out to a fancy neighborhood on the northwest side of Chicago and join the stream of cars ogling at the fancy lights and mechanized displays on the homes and lawns.

Hanukkah was a fairly mellow event, or I assume it was since I do not remember much beyond this one fact: our family mixed the latke batter in the blender rather than grating the potatoes. I didn't understand the distinction until I was older and, I must admit, I have since joined the grating team. I loved standing watch at the electric griddle on the kitchen table while Mom manned the stovetop. Most of the menorahs, or more correctly *hanukkiot*, in our home were made of tin, practically disposable, and obtained from the synagogue. We did have one family menorah my grandparents brought from Israel. *Gelt?* Gifts? Likely we had some, but there was nothing fancy going on there.

As an adult, I found my relationship to Hanukkah ebbed and flowed depending on the community I lived in, my attachment and access to Jewish community, and my general state of mind. Hanukkah was typically approached as a children's holiday, and I neither was one nor had one nor often had other childless adults or families with whom I was close and with whom I might celebrate. As I became more serious about Judaism, Hanukkah became more commercial. I still remember being surprised the first time I saw *hanukkiot* and candles, along with special latke platters and twinkling Hanukkah lights, at the big-box stores. I wasn't delighted. Rarely shopping at large chains to begin with, I made a special effort to source my Judaica from more appropriate places.

As my values evolved so did my enjoyment of the public face of Christmas. Living close to the neighborhood in Flagstaff that hosted the annual light show, I would walk by and think: "Wow, I wonder how many unrenewable energy resources are being wasted on *that one*." But I am not a total scrooge. There was a very sweet, animated rendition of Santa's workshop in a nearby garage that somehow managed to touch me each year, and I still enjoy the beauty of creative and simple lights in the dark nights.

When I met Jon, I was rather shocked to hear that he, too, grew up going to movies and Chinese food on Christmas day. Somehow, that tradition dovetailed with his family's Christmas celebration, as an addition to it rather than an "instead of." This was not really relevant to our potential as partners, but fun nonetheless. By the time we met, his religious and personal values had transformed very much, as mine had. I know that moving into my house that fall provided the perfect excuse for him to finally stop getting a tree for his kids.

Each year at Hanukkah we have host friends for ethnically themed Hanukkah celebrations, with egg rolls or pakoras standing in for the ubiquitous latkes. The year we moved from Vermont to Chicago, not far from my parents, the sense of having our life in transition was a big inspiration for us during Hanukkah, and we took time each evening watching the candles and discussing to what we should be dedicating ourselves in this new situation, ultimately seeking involvement in a local homeless program. Sima participated for the first time, not quite understanding that on Hanukkah she didn't need to cover her eyes after the candles were lit, a tradition she learned from our weekly Shabbat observance.

Our challenge was sharing the experience with my family. For decades, my parents have hosted their local children and grandchildren for an annual Hanukkah party. Despite my parents' efforts to raise their daughters within Judaism, this may be the only Jewish activity their guests partake in each year. We negotiated hard to move the party off Shabbat afternoon, but compromised in the end. So we went, but

bowed out early in order to give Sima a nap prior to going to our little synagogue's Hanukkah party. There we made *havdalah* **to mark the end of Shabbat, lit a dozen** *hanukkiot,* **sang traditional songs, and were grateful for the miracles in our lives.**

Holidays happen all year round, and they can be either opportunities for discovery or sources of stress for interfaith couples and families. They will be what you make of them.

Every religious tradition has its holidays. Some happen only once a year: Bodhi Day for Buddhists, for example, when the enlightenment of the Buddha is celebrated, is a time when your Buddhist loved one may spend all day in meditation, study, and celebration. In many parts of the world, by the way, this is also a December holiday—on December 8!

Other holidays may not feel so much like holidays if you are simply watching from the "outside." If you are coupled with a Muslim, for instance, and don't share his or her faith, Ramadan can prove a serious challenge—unless you come to understand it. Fasting is central and important in Islam, and if you are in an intimate relationship with a Muslim you will likely come to appreciate what this and other practices mean to your partner. You may even surprise yourself and find yourself joining in. There are many good reasons, spiritual and otherwise, to not eat between sunup and sundown. Perhaps you will discover yours.

CHAPTER 8

———

Creating a House of Faith

A beautiful scene of "coming home" is modeled in Frank Capra's classic 1946 film, *It's a Wonderful Life*. Mary and George Bailey, played by Donna Reed and Jimmy Stewart, present a family of new homeowners with three traditional gifts: bread, for sustenance; salt, for flavor; and wine, for joy. The symbolism evokes a sense that home life can be simple, meaningful, hopeful. That the Baileys also made a personal investment allowing the Martinis to secure their home points to the importance of relationships with community, homes connected with other homes. We are all intertwined with each other, despite our differences.

How do we consciously bring our faith into the homes we create? Across religious traditions, a handful of values seem to characterize this abode including generosity, gratitude, and hospitality, represented by acts of charity, blessings, and prayer, and the welcoming of friends and strangers alike. The presence of religious symbols in the home, such as a cross on the wall or a *mezuzah* on the doorpost, often remind us of the intentions within. A dedicated bookshelf, icon corner, extra room reserved for an altar and meditation cushion, or simple prayer rug creates space for religious thought and practice.

JON I've often wondered how Michal escaped the "pithy sign" gene. Her parents' and sisters' homes exhibit scattered plaques, posters, and magnets, some cynical, some inspirational, some with lists of "life's little instructions." But when I first met Michal the only words on her walls, other than an ordination certificate, were in a rendering of a verse of Psalms, painted by a colleague for the cover of her rabbinic graduation program. When I inquired about it, she explained that the Hebrew translates, "I will sing to God with my life." Now, she and I have a second sign, a wedding gift from one of my oldest colleagues; it is a bronze-colored plaque engraved with words of Erasmus, made famous by C. G. Jung, and now hangs in our bedroom: "Bidden or unbidden, God is present."

Both of these point to a single theme—that the way we live in our homes should reflect the presence of faith. This concept, and the values and ethics it suggests to us, influences our speech and our actions, our use of finances and resources.

Actually there is a third sign, my first gift to Michal, which I acquired while we were dating and I was visiting a friend in New Orleans. It's a piece of hand-painted folk art that resembles a sandwich board. Bright and cartoonish ten-inch-tall white-on-red letters proclaim "Shalom Y'all!" I loved the piece immediately, but it is funky, so I wondered during the entire return flight whether or not Michal would appreciate it. Her first reaction when opening the wrapping paper was to remark that it didn't blend at all in style or tone with anything else that she owned. But it did not take long for her to find a perfect place for it in her, soon to become our, front entryway.

That greeting still evokes the hospitality that we aspire to, as well as our openness to all, including multiple religious traditions. Hanging nearby are some smaller bits of popular art, including a colorful drawing of a bright blue Krishna given to me by a friend from Nepal, a papyrus boldly painted with the Egyptian creation myth that Michal acquired in Cairo, a striking black-and-white duotone of a whirling dervish that appeared in my first book back in 2000, and a framed greeting card featuring a seated yogi, composed completely of bits of flora, chosen by Michal for herself years ago. It still makes her smile.

Rhythms of time and season frame for us ways of appreciating and connecting to God, faith, and tradition at home. For many people, including perhaps most interfaith couples, the "prime time" seasons are religious holidays like Ramadan, Passover, and Christmas. These are important, of course, but perhaps inevitable. Whether they are experienced as deeply spiritual holy days, festive family meals, or something in between will depend on the intention brought to them.

In contrast are the daily rhythms that form the core of

many home practices. Meditation, prayer, yoga, or spiritual reading early in the morning or before bed are common ways to ground the day and connect with faith and spirit. Some couples, and families with children, establish a regular practice of one or many of them. Other partners may decide to begin the day, one with yoga, the other in prayer, and then come together for a different, joint practice a little while later. Whatever your style, establishing a practice of any sort will infuse your home with divine goodness.

The table where we eat is a central place of activity in every home, and it can become a profoundly spiritual place, too. There's no place better than the table to invite friends and strangers (new friends) to come. And mealtime blessings provide moments of connection and gratitude. Our Christian-Muslim friends, Wendy and Ahmed, alternate in offering blessings from their respective traditions. Mindy and Bob, who come from Jewish and Christian families but now identify as nones, lead their children in a beautiful blessing of gratitude to the four elements that we've experienced at our dinner table. Each of these moments can be as simple as they are powerful in the impact they have when inserted in a hectic or difficult day.

Perhaps the most essential rhythm of all, in both Judaism and Christianity, is the ancient tradition of a weekly Sabbath. While celebrated in widely varying ways across denominations, the Sabbath day offers a focus that is different from the rest of the week. Put most simply, gratitude, praise, and ceasing replace wanting, planning, and working. With such qualities to recommend it, one wonders why a Sabbath day is not more widely observed. As a matter of fact, we often hear from others that stepping back from work or running errands for a day would simply make life too difficult.

Years ago, Michal read an article in a natural health magazine about a Chicago area cancer specialist. He had a full-time clinical practice and a teaching position at a local university, and he ran an alternative healing center. And he was an Orthodox Jew. "How can you accomplish all of that and take a day off?" the editors asked him. He answered, "The day of rest and reflection is what allows me to do what I do." We understand his point and find that stopping for a day provides perspective, balance, and time for reflection. While this type of practice is most common in Jewish circles, Seventh-day Adventists usually observe a Sabbath day regularly, and there has been some recent resurgence in exploring a more complete day of rest in other Christians' lives as well.[21]

One day a week we turn off our computers (ahhh!) and dedicate time to prayer, study, connecting with family and friends, and, occasionally, reading something frivolous that we didn't have time to enjoy during the week. Shabbat renews our relationships with each other at home. Throughout the week we work together a great deal, but from Friday night to Saturday early evening we spend our time together eating with friends, praying together in synagogue, taking long walks, giving Sima the attention she deserves, sneaking the occasional nap, and even spending other sorts of time together in bed (you get spiritual brownie points for it on this day, according to the ancient rabbis).

In addition to this essential weekly rhythm marker, there

are also everyday preoccupations that make up our attempts to live rightly. Take food, for instance. Islam, Judaism, various traditions of Buddhism, Hinduism, and other Eastern traditions, as well as Seventh-day Adventists have specific guidelines regarding how and what food may be prepared and enjoyed. Bringing consciousness to the food we eat and serve in our homes provides constant connection to a tradition. That connection, as well as the practice of offering blessings over food, reminds us of the spiritual, natural, and human sources of our sustenance. Thich Nhat Hanh summarizes this beautifully in his well-known table contemplation: "This food is the gift of the whole universe....May we eat with mindfulness and gratitude so as to be worthy to receive it."

MICHAL Our progressive understanding of God and tradition tends to translate and expand timeless concepts into some specific practices in our home. We are primarily vegetarians, and rather than looking for marks that food is *kosher*, we strive to buy local, organic, and non-commercial foods whenever possible. Our respect for creation motivates us to reuse and recycle, to swap or purchase secondhand, to walk, bike, or use public transportation whenever possible. We of course aren't alone in this. Numerous faith-based groups recognize their religious traditions as the basis for choosing sustainable living.[22]

Religion is a central aspect of our lives and a resident in our home. Our practices and belongings reflect our sense of God's presence in our lives. Generosity, hospitality, and gratitude all point us to own less, spend less, share more, live simply. To some, the choices we make, especially the ways we don't participate in the dominant, surrounding culture, might appear regressive. We are finding many others who are doing what we are trying to do: live sustainably, perhaps even practice downward mobility. What we don't own, eat, or purchase makes us a bit unusual, we realize, but we embrace it. At every turn, we experience life as rich and meaningful, and don't feel that we are lacking.

The idea of providing hospitality remains important to Jon and me, and we enjoy extending invitations to others and welcoming friends of friends or other visitors to accept our gift of a comfortable place to stay. Ultimately, this impulse points to a larger vision we have. We imagine a day when we may share a large house or cluster of homes with others with whom we share values and priorities, living in community. This would further reduce our personal level of consumption and ownership, leaving more of what we have to share, and enrich the non-material aspects of our lives tremendously, like creating extended family. And there would always be room for the sojourner, whether friend or stranger.

"There's *no* place like *home!*" Dorothy exclaims at the climax of *The Wizard of Oz*, which Michal quotes endlessly and believes is the cinematic magnum opus of 20th-century secular religion. (Michal also has ruby slippers and can sing the part, but we digress.) There is indeed no place quite like home—when we make our homes places that nurture and sustain our desires and values spiritually and religiously. This requires attention; it doesn't happen as a matter of course. In fact, what usually happens, instead, is that the urgent matter of the moment takes precedent, and as we all know, there is always an urgent matter of the moment.

For Oz's Dorothy, discovering that she wanted to be home meant recognizing the beauty and value of what she already had. The joke on her, of course, was that the colorful, exotic characters that led her back home were the very same folk who inhabited her seeming black-and-white world. The sources for your own spiritual home-making are likely close at hand, waiting to be reinvigorated.

———

CHAPTER 9

Visiting God's House

MICHAL "I cried at mass this morning," Jon said. "Sometimes I just want to connect to God *so* much, it gets very powerful." I suspect this was the only conversation of its kind occurring on the cardio floor of the McGaw YMCA that morning, as we sat on adjoining recumbent bicycles.

Jon and I have shared to the best of our ability our personal experiences during prayer and ritual. I think he is better at expressing this than I am. Nothing has been more powerful than his description of taking communion, of taking God into his body, of satisfying his spiritual hunger. And for whatever reason, I don't find this strange or upsetting, even if the ritual is somewhat foreign.

So by the first time I joined Jon at mass, after he abandoned his commitment to our local but absolutely too conservative parish, I understood a bit of what to expect, or at least what I could imagine. I was *mostly* comfortable that first morning, even as I remained seated while everyone else kneeled and later as Jon filtered into the line for Eucharist. I watched the parishoners cycle through the church: filing forward, kneeling, returning to their pews, and I noticed the looks on their faces. I didn't make eye contact with Jon as he returned to his spot, but as he knelt again next to me, head lowered on his fisted hands, what welled up in me was "I love this man."

"*Mah tovu* . . . How fair are your tents, O Jacob, your encampments, O Israel!" This exclamation is found in the book of Numbers (24:5), rendered by the prophet Balaam. Known in biblical lore mostly for his talking donkey (two chapters before), this is where Balaam explains to his king, Balak, that he is unable to curse the Israelites, as Balak had wanted him to do, because he can only follow God's instructions.

"How beautiful are your tents. . . . your dwelling places" is Balaam reflecting on two types of space that he saw when he observed the camps of the tribes of Israel: tents that housed the families, and the *mishkan*—or tabernacle—the dwelling place for God's presence in the community. God did not necessarily reside, or reside only, in the *mishkan*, but as God tells Moses earlier in the Torah, "Have them make me a sanctuary, so that I may dwell among them" (Exodus 25:8). They did build it, and to very precise specifications. The *mishkan* was the site of the ritual sacrifices that were the core of the ancient Israelite religion, but even more so, it was a gathering place and a reminder of the divine presence wherever they went. (Imagine the end of the first Indiana Jones movie, but without the melting faces.)

We all create tents and encampments, our family homes

and neighborhoods, but we need other homes as well, spiritual gathering places where we can meet together in faith, practice the rituals that enhance our lives, and be surrounded by a community of similar values. These places dedicated to religious practice and divine presence are where we pray, learn, reflect, play, eat, praise, and connect with others. These are also spaces where we feel safe bringing our failings, questions, and doubts, because we know that they, too, will be heard without judgment.

We need these. And like the ancient *mishkan* created by the Israelites, our religious practices and connections transcend the walls and doors of buildings. When a church or synagogue or mosque does all this well, the impact flows back into the broader community, as well as right back into our homes. And, as Michal will suggest to a congregation as the morning service begins with the singing of *Mah tovu*, it is the presence and intention of a gathered community that turns any space into a holy dwelling.

During a meditation, mass, prayer service, or other ritual, multiple dynamics can be happening. We are praying or participating in some way and likely having a personal, spiritual experience. We are also hearing and seeing one another, connecting to our partner, if they are there next to us, and to the community around us. And we are connecting *as a community* to the intention and tradition that bind us together. For Buddhists, this may occur during a *metta* meditation. For Muslims, it might be in responding to the midday call for prayer. For Christians, the recitation of the Lord's Prayer, often while holding hands, can mark this sort of moment. For Jews, it may be the recitation of the *Shema* prayer, or a communal *aliyah*, the blessing for reading from the Torah scroll. We all have our beautiful moments!

When we initially outlined all the material we wanted to cover in *Mixed-Up Love*, our notes for this chapter focused on the importance and value of finding a spiritual community—a temple, church, mosque, and so on. But by the time we began to write the chapter, having spoken to dozens of couples, many of whom you've already "met" in these pages, we discovered that this is one of the places where the rubber really meets the road in interfaith relationships. If planning a marriage ceremony is the point when many couples first encounter their religious differences in an intimate way, choosing a house of prayer together is where we often feel disappointment or frustration—not necessarily in each other, but in the innate limitations of our situations. Couples with connections to different traditions don't always pray easily together in community. The word we have heard, more often than we anticipated, was "lonely." And frankly, it was only after we sat with so many others, talking about *their* experiences, that we realized that a part of our own experience echoed their disappointment.

Wendy and Ahmed, for instance, are more likely to visit their respective church and mosque alone. Exceptions to this rule are major Christian holidays and the Fridays when Ahmed visits his mother's grave, near a mosque farther from home. At these moments they attend as a couple, providing each other with support and companionship. At the mosque, Wendy is in the woman's section and not quite able to take in the experience in Arabic, but she likes being there with her spouse. Yet, most of the time, their religious experiences in community are as individuals.

Lainie, our Wiccan friend in Vermont, finds being in her spouse's Unitarian-Universalist church difficult, as the setting and mostly intellectual language feels limited compared to the nature-based approach that characterizes her own spiritual tradition. She feels like she would do better in a Catholic church, in which she was raised and which feels more spiritual to her. So for now, Sunday morning has become dad and son time, which provides much-needed quiet and space for Lainie, but certainly doesn't enhance their marriage or family life.

We determined early on that our family practice would be Jewish—in the home, and congregationally. This didn't preclude Michal's joining Jon at church, but even at that first mass, described previously, Michal had difficulties. As she listened to the sermon based on the story of the patriarch Joseph, she responded in a way that has since become something of a theme in our conversations: "Don't you have your *own* stories you can use from the altar?" It is difficult for a Jew to hear the essential texts of her tradition reinterpreted for different purposes by another tradition, often declared as Truth. (The fact that the Hebrew Bible remains an essential part of the Christian canon can also be a source of confusion for *Christians*, who also don't necessarily realize that what they are hearing is *not* modern Judaism.) As a rabbi, Michal intellectually understands why stories like the miraculous crossing of the Red Sea remain an inspiration for Christians, but emotionally she still wants to stand up during the homily at Jon's mass and say, "Leave my texts alone!"

Also memorable for us, going back to one of our earliest shared religious experiences, was the time we took Jon's older kids to Christmas Eve mass. We'd only been together as a family for a few months. Michal sat, listened, and enjoyed hearing the singing of a teen she knew from other local activities in town. Jon's son Joe pretty much fell asleep, or pretended that he was. And his daughter, Clelia, sat reading the book she'd brought with her, showing no intention whatsoever of listening to the service.

An hour and a half later, as we walked far enough away from the doors of the church to be out of earshot of others, we debriefed. "Really boring," was Joe's appraisal, followed by Clelia, with decidedly more emotion: "How can people say things that they *know* they can't possibly believe?!" And Michal: "I still don't quite understand why you need Jesus if you have God." For his part, Jon had a meaningful experience and the post-game critiques didn't seem to affect that much at all. So if we are any indication of a norm, visiting God's house together can be a mixed bag.

From what we have heard, we suspect that these experiences are somewhat typical. Teenagers of any background are, of course, rarely the most religiously open and interested demographic group, a result of simple neurobiology perhaps. And Jews, as well as other non-Christians, tend to have more difficulty in churches than the other way around. As our Christian friend Gerry once shared, "Before Leslie [his Jewish wife] and I met, I feel that I had become almost a 'Jewish-Christian,' who spent more time in the prophets and psalms than in the Gospels. For Leslie, Christianity is foreign; but for me, Judaism feels almost like a second home. It deepens my faith."

The third and last time we went to church together as

a couple, we actually up and left in the middle. The message being communicated that day throughout the readings, and then the homily, was clear (the Gospel of John figured prominently): there is one way, you are out or in, and being out is pretty awful. Michal left, Jon followed.

This imbalance is a result of how Judaism and Christianity relate to one another historically and liturgically: Christianity essentially absorbed much of the faith and then built a new tradition upon it. A similar situation can exist between the religious traditions when a Jew or Christian is with a Muslim, or, for example, when a Protestant or Catholic is dating a Mormon. Shia and Sunni Muslims, and Sikhs partnering with Hindus, easily encounter these problems in various forms, too. When one tradition supersedes another, it can feel exclusive. So, a non-Jew may easily feel "lost" in Jewish liturgy, as we most often pray in a language that is foreign to them, but a non-Christian can easily feel insulted at a Christian service, and in plain English.

Some couples find creative ways to compromise when their respective traditions don't agree. Our friend Eboo Patel and his wife do this, as they come from two different strands of Islam that can feel exclusive at times, even to other Muslims. As Eboo explained, "Roughly speaking, we face something like a Catholic-Protestant issue. Ismailis have a pope figure, the Aga Khan. And Sunnis believe in the text, the Qur'an, and the example of the Prophet, without any current human figure. What we do is find where we overlap the most. Our prayers are often different, but they are also often the same—so we focus on those. And then we hold on to the particulars that really matter to us."

We have had our own bit of loneliness, or at least Jon has. Churchgoing hasn't been easy for Michal—or at least it wasn't in the early going of our relationship. And now that we live near a progressive parish that Michal would like to experience, Jon tends to want to be at mass only and especially on week- days at 7:30 in the morning, when Michal and Sima are usually still in bed. So for the time being, mass remains Jon's private experience in our relationship. It can feel lonely not to be shar- ing it in some way. Jon doesn't so much want Michal to experi- ence what he experiences (that won't happen), but he wants to be sure that she knows how it is important to him. She does.

Naomi Schaefer Riley reports in her recent book about inter- faith marriage on the level of marital satisfaction as it relates to a couple's rate of church attendance together. Couples with equal commitments to church attendance are happier than those with significant differences, and marital satisfac- tion is lowest for the more religiously involved spouse.[23]

To address that problem, there is a program in greater Washington, D.C., where Jewish-Christian interfaith fam- ilies gather regularly for dual education, ritual celebration, and worship. The Interfaith Families Project of Greater Washington brings together more than one hundred families from Maryland, Virginia, and the District and, in their own words, "seeks to develop our children, ourselves, and our community in an environment that encourages questions and respects different answers. IFFP provides opportunities for education about Christianity and Judaism, holiday cel- ebrations, fellowship, spiritual gatherings, community ser- vice, and exploration of interfaith identity."[24]

IFFP meets on Sunday mornings at a Maryland high school for what they call the "Gathering" (similar to a worship service), as well as adult education, Sunday school for the kids, and a yoga class. The community is diverse in their approach to religious practice, as stated on the IFFP website: "Our community includes those who continue to practice a faith, and those who do not. Many IFFP parents have chosen not to select one religion for their children, but rather to instill in them an appreciation and understanding of both heritages. Other IFFP parents have chosen one religion for their children but want them to gain knowledge about both of their cultural heritages." Beyond the education and programming, the most potentially valuable thing this program provides is community for families trying to integrate their spiritual paths in some cohesive way.

Deciding early on that our family and communal religious practice would be singular certainly simplified figuring out some of these details. Still, we go through some of the same processes that every couple goes through, even as we navigate where we will happily pray together on Shabbat morning.

Because we have moved several times since our relationship began, we have done a bunch of *shul*-hopping. And whenever we enter a new congregation we have different antennae active. Michal tends to be most responsive to the way the leaders involve the community ritually and the content of a service, while Jon is very sensitive to the community itself, the effort made in welcoming and including, and their tolerance for our young child. He also notices the level of diversity within a congregation, a value he highly esteems. And of course, we need to be welcomed as an interfaith couple and Michal must be considered acceptable as a rabbi, even with Jon as "*rebbitzman*."[25]

Life within a congregation, the give and take that both feeds us and allows us to contribute to something greater than ourselves, is essential to our spiritual lives, like oxygen and carbon dioxide moving in and out of our bodies. But it is sometimes the case that one partner feels like he or she has "lost," while the other partner has "won," in the religious wrestling match of where to worship or in what tradition to most often pray. Wherever you decide to practice your faith together as a couple, it is important to communicate well, be candid, and honest.

JON There are times when I actually enjoy feeling like a spiritual outsider, as when I've spent hours at the back of a monastery church while the monks chant psalms from their tight corrals, or when I've sat alone in a side chapel of a big inner-city church where I know not a soul. I feel simultaneously alone, connected to God, and part of a very large community of seekers at those moments. Strange, isn't it, how anonymity can breed those feelings all at once? But it can.

But I take more sustenance from time spent among friends, or at least with people who recognize me and know my name, with whom I've prayed and worshipped before. In other words, a congregation. I want to be a part of a community of prayer. The fact that my congregation is now Jewish/synagogue rather than Christian/church is just fine. I feel fortunate to have such a diverse range of experiences with God.

Prayer is, for me, a basic instinct, not quite like breathing, but as natural as, say, jumping out of the way of a moving car. I pray like that, sometimes, in sudden bursts of need and thankfulness. But most powerful for me, whether I'm at mass or in *shul*, is when liturgy, community, and spirit combine to feed and make possible my sense of praise and gratitude to God.

In recent years, I've been inspired by the *siddurim*, or prayer books, that I've learned to use in synagogue. "Morning Blessings" is usually what comes first in a Saturday morning service, and those prayers contain the essence of my feelings of gratefulness and need. Everything is right there in the most basic and exhilarating language of human desire and response. Most familiar of all (to Jews at least) is the prayer of reverence and awe that we spoke of previously, called *Mah tovu*, or "How lovely." This old prayer weaves together Bible verses from the books of Numbers and Psalms and includes these beautiful lines:

How lovely are your tents
Drawn by your love, I come into your house
I fall in prayer
I greet, I bless, I bend the knee, before The One
   who fashions me.

Then begins the reciting of a long litany of blessings. In succession, they acknowledge the God, life of all the worlds, who removes the sleep from our eyes, who makes the blind to see, who clothes the naked, who sets the captive free, who makes firm a person's steps, who made me in the divine image. For all of those things and more, I am both needy and grateful.

CHAPTER 10

Blessing Our Children

JON I brought two children to my relationship with Michal. Clelia and Joe are both in college today, but back then they were splitting time equally between their mom and dad. They were great kids, and are now talented young adults beginning lives on their own, but neither has a religious life today. By the time they were teenagers it was clear that, despite being a religiously passionate and participating father, I did not successfully transmit much to them. I've reflected often on why that may have happened.

Clelia and Joe were raised in a progressive Christian home. I taught no catechism, and my kids learned that a religious or spiritual path is valid only if it helps to make you a good person. They grew up in the Episcopal church. They knew a lot of Sunday morning services, coffee hours, Easter vigils, Shrove Tuesday pancake suppers, choir performances, and summer church fairs, but being in a small and rural congregation, they had little to no Sunday school. Nevertheless, they had plenty of organized religion; the problem was their parents failed to bring religion home in meaningful ways.

It saddens me that today they have no understanding of what faith, God, and religion can do for them, how it can instruct the emotions, feed the spirit, inspire the mind, and create community. All they really remember are some decent pot-lucks. That was my fault.

I did little to model religious practice or spiritual exercise in front of my kids, outside of church. When I prayed or medi-tated, I was almost always somewhere else. When I was vol-unteering, I was usually on my own. Spiritual retreats and writing spiritual books were my own private experiences.

So when Michal and I married, even before we decided to have a baby, I knew that I'd want to tie together organized reli-gion, personal faith, and life at home in ways that I missed the first time around. Now, I figured, I had the chance to do it better.

For many of us in interfaith couplings, the hiccup of reli-gious discussion that erupts as we move in together, or plan our wedding or commitment ceremonies, settles down for a while…sometimes a very long while. We may continue to practice our faith(s), or not to, as a couple or as individuals, depending on our personal level of interest in bringing faith into the home. And this often lasts right up until the arrival of children, actual or imagined, into our lives.

Then, a new round of discussion begins: How will we raise the kids? In what tradition(s)? With what religious identity? Will they receive religious education? As our friend Leslie, a Jew who married a mainline Protestant in her late fifties, a second marriage for both, wisely remarked: "Not having any possibility of children takes away a whole basketful of issues!" So true.

All of those considerations you made while planning your wedding—your religious identities and preferences, the messages you carry from your upbringings, the desire for support from and connection to your families of origin—are now returning in spades. And the choices you make now will have a much stronger and longer impact on your life, and your children's lives, than a one-time wedding ceremony.

If this is the situation you find yourself in, know that you have plenty of company. You certainly can expect to hear people say you should have considered these issues before ever deciding to tie the knot. (We probably said that to you, in fact, a few chapters earlier.) Not discussing these things up front is a little like falling in love with a house, finding a great mortgage, and closing before realizing the fact that the boundary for the primary school you liked was across the street.

This is why many clergy who work with intermarrying couples will ask you to try exploring this, and other decisions about religious life, before the wedding happens. Our friend Dr. Phil Amerson, who recently retired as the president of Garrett-Evangelical Theology Seminary, explains how he learned this only through trial and error, midway in his career as a United Methodist pastor. After watching couples he married trip up later over religious issues in their marriages, he eventually determined that he would only marry those who were willing to work with him in a meaningful way up front. They had to be able to imagine and address the potential complications of an interfaith family life, including achieving some clarity on raising children.

Sometimes resolution of these issues is mandatory, as it is, for instance, if you would like to be married in a mosque or a Catholic church. Muslim law permits Muslim men to marry only certain non-Muslim women; Muslim women may not intermarry at all. In all cases, the children of marriages performed within the faith are presumed to be Muslim.

And it was not long ago that Catholic canonical language referred to couples comprised of one Catholic and one baptized Protestant as "of mixed religion." Before changes to canon law in 1983, written promises to raise their children as Catholics were required from both partners if they wanted to be married in the Catholic Church. Now, only the Catholic member has to sign a statement that it is their *intention* to raise Catholic children, without reference to the other partner. Still, regardless of the official forms sent to the diocesan office, the priest has the obligation to help a couple understand what this decision will mean for their family and the advantage of considering it in advance, for the benefit of all involved.

Despite all of this preparation, don't worry if these issues are now fresh in your minds. You are, again, in good company. Even if you had all the answers when you were dating, or when you were in pre-marital counseling, when the actual time comes for kids, questions or doubts may rear their heads again. Even having had great clarity back then doesn't guarantee that you won't begin to second-guess yourselves by the time your baby begins to call you "Mama" or "Dada." Feelings of nostalgia, responsibility, heritage, or a combination of all of these, may suddenly set in.

Our Wiccan friend Lainie certainly had that experience when she became a mother. Not only did she have some vague sense of wanting to return to her roots, but she found that she now was resonating with her Catholic memories of the Virgin Mary in her maternal role, beseeching her in moments of needful prayer. And she missed the sense of community in which she was raised.

It is not uncommon for one or both partners to be surprised to find that their own religious attachments and desires unexpectedly surface with the arrival of children. Sometimes a death in the family, or some other personal tragedy, will awaken religious feelings that had lain dormant even before the arrival of children. And what had felt like not a big deal can suddenly become one. In this case, there can be feelings ranging from confusion to betrayal that might make working through the issue anew potentially more difficult than the process of deciding which way to go early on.

How couples approach the question of raising children usually falls in line with their own religious involvement. Many interfaith couples include one nominal member of a tradition and another who is more significantly involved. Others, still, include one partner who is not religious at all. This is sometimes simply a result of history: one person grew up in a religious family, while the other did not. Or sometimes the family was religious but the individual's interest, practice, or identity has lapsed, or vice versa. So, when they meet someone of a different faith background, there is little conflict between them on religious issues, and once kids arrive, one agrees to raise the kids in the other's religion.

An event occurred recently in Michal's family, with her nephew, that illustrates this situation, as well as some of the things to think about if you are that couple. It began with a worried call from her parents.

"Melissa wants to have Jonah baptized. Ben isn't sure what to say. We are, of course, very uncomfortable with the idea," they said on the phone.

A Catholic of Puerto Rican descent, Melissa is committed to Catholicism and is active in her parish, having chosen to be confirmed in the Church as an adult. Ben was brought up with no religious affiliation or education. Technically, he was Jewish through his mother, but neither of his parents was interested in religion. While they were dating, Melissa was surprised and concerned about Ben's lack of Jewish knowledge, and even wondered whether he, and their son, might establish a connection to his Jewish heritage.

But when baby Jonah arrived, Melissa assumed that he would be baptized. Church was an important and meaningful aspect of her life, closely tied to her family and community. Ben had no objections. He was, after all, giving up nothing.

Soon after Jonah's birth we met with Melissa and Ben for breakfast. They were surprised and relieved to find that not only did we not question their plan, but we wholly supported it. What perfect sense it made to us to have the child of an involved Catholic mother and an essentially secular father be baptized. How good it would be for Jonah to be initiated into a vital religious tradition that might help to inspire his life toward good things and provide connection to community and family.

Michal's parents' discomfort at having a Christian great-grandchild is not unusual. They considered their grandson Jewish by descent, through his mother, even without education or participation, and they felt the loss of Jonah's Jewish identity deeply. (Never mind that, according to this line of reasoning, Jonah was *not* Jewish.) They asked Ben, and us, whether Jonah should have a Hebrew baby naming or other Jewish welcoming ceremony, but they eventually grasped why that wouldn't make sense under the circumstances.

Jonah will likely have some exposure to Judaism, just as his father and uncles had, joining Michal's parents, and perhaps some of his cousins, for Jewish holidays and family events. Someday he, and even his father, may decide to explore Judaism in some way. But for now, giving Jonah and the family a spiritual home with depth and meaning seems a gift that he shouldn't be denied.

Our friend and Catholic priest Father Bob Oldershaw has a similar perspective, and his advice makes good sense. He says, "I had a clergy friend who would counsel interfaith couples using what he called the valence theory: Which way are they leaning? Who has the greater inertia, to which tradition? That then is the way in which a couple should go."

Then there are couples with two partners who are each invested in their respective traditions, wishing to raise the kids in both religions simultaneously. The challenge in this scenario, of course, comes if one partner is not fully open to the other's tradition. It would be extremely difficult to make things work under such circumstances—at least with any real intimacy or transparency—if one partner believed that his or her religious path held the one and only truth. An inter-religious or inter-church family would find it nearly impossible unless both parents were committed to some form of progressive understanding of faith itself, an understanding that respects the validity of multiple ways.

Assuming mutual religious respect, then, a truly inter-religious or inter-church home will succeed to the extent in which everyone is committed and honest, and perhaps, the extent to which the investment of the two parents is fair and balanced.

Couples in which both members have minimal or no religious involvement might be perfectly comfortable doing a modicum of religious observance of two faiths with their children. They may participate in the major holidays of both traditions, with their extended families or in the home. In most cases, none of the practices or symbols will take on significant spiritual meaning, which means that there is also less potential for conflict—even though potential difficulties with grandparents and other family members remain.

But then, as interest and commitment to a particular tradition increase, things get more interesting and involved. Our friends Rachel and Jeremy, for instance, offer a striking example of parents who are equally invested in teaching their children their faiths (Protestantism and Judaism, respectively), but they run into conflict around how to blend seemingly contradictory ritual observances. Their daughter was both blessed at church and formally converted to Judaism. They practice Judaism mainly at home, not having found a synagogue that feels right for them, and they attend a small church regularly. Most Sunday mornings when Jeremy is at church he will tend to stay outside the sanctuary with the kids, avoiding the somewhat uncomfortable ritual. And then when Jeremy is not around, Rachel has their young daughter take communion. Clearly there is some disconnect here and they're working on resolving it. But how will these disparate pieces be joined in a way that creates a sense of wholeness for their daughter and for the family? They don't yet know.

Similarly, our friend Eboo and his wife have to navigate coming from two distinct branches of Islam. His community has a prayer hall that is closed to non-Ismailis, so she cannot come. Still, as Eboo says, "There are a set of Ismaili things that I do on my own and that I will take our kids to." In addition, the family has enrolled the kids in an Islamic education program unrelated to either of their specific branches of faith, providing a shared religious foundation relevant to both traditions.

In Chicago there is an experiential interfaith project called Family School. Now in its twentieth year, the school hosts a weekly Sunday program for Jewish-Catholic children and their parents, with a dual curriculum that integrates major topics and teachings from both faith traditions. These families go deeper than simply observing the major religious holidays. They are developing religious literacy while exploring two traditions at once. How deeply into practice and theology these families delve varies tremendously, and it is unclear how or if the program can help resolve any difficulties that some families might experience as they attempt to incorporate two full sets of religious ritual into their family lives or try to understand what they mean when they say "God."

Also in Chicago is an organization called the Interfaith Union, which runs two schools based on the family school model and offers a unique joint Jewish baby naming and Catholic baptism service. As Eileen O'Farrell Smith, an originator and advocate of this dual-ritual observance, explains in her book:

> Since 1991, families and clergy have created and celebrated ceremonies to welcome and bless our children in a religious context with a Catholic Priest and Rabbi as Co-Presiders. These ceremonies are spiritual moments, created in the spirit of finding new pathways for interfaith families to share their traditions. For some couples, their ceremony makes the statement about the religious identity of their child, either in one faith tradition or another, or sometimes both. For others, it is an expression of thanks to God for new life and the wish to beseech God's blessing on their family. Our goal is to respond to each family and to help them discover a ritual that is authentic to their own vision of faith and life.[26]

At the end of Smith's book is a transcript of an interview with a priest and a rabbi that are involved with Interfaith Union. While they describe the novelty of their endeavor and the resistance to it in conventional religious settings, they also address the "why" of doing such a dual-tradition ceremony. Both clergy conclude that performing a ritual without the intention of living Christian and Jewish lives, without being part of a synagogue and a parish, simply doesn't make sense. We wholeheartedly agree with one part of their conclusion—to do a ceremony without it leading to a life of meaningful practice seems empty.

For a perspective on all of this we spoke to Rabbi Isaac Serotta, a Reform rabbi in suburban Chicago who has worked with Interfaith Union for several years, originally as a rabbinic consultant and teacher to the families involved in the schools. Rabbi Ike, as his congregants call him, has recently begun facilitating the baptism/baby naming ceremonies. He explained: "If they had asked me to do that at the beginning, I would have said no. But that isn't how it started. And then, when I saw what they were doing, I decided that this path they are on has an honor of its own. It is their unique thing that they are creating and I don't know what it will be."

Rabbi Serotta went on to suggest that the instruction the children receive is likely different from what they would find in a strictly Jewish or Catholic school, pointing more to stories and values and less to theologies or dogmas that would be contradictory or confusing. Also, for the most part, he explained, the families don't have relationships with other religious institutions or clergy, and the bulk of their Jewish practice takes place in the home.

Serotta admits that this aspect of his rabbinic practice remains a bit "edgy" for him, but finds himself continuing to go deeper with these families. He reflected, "Most interfaith couples don't do anything—so the fact that you have these couples trying to figure out what religious path is right for them and their family should be honored and recognized as counter-cultural to what's typical. Faith is important to them. They are struggling with it all in ways that other interfaith couples are not. They realize that they are modeling an openness of faith. We used to raise kids with simply, 'You were born this,' and that's it. But they are following a path that says faith is a journey. Their parents are preparing them to be on a faith journey more than most parents are."

The fact is that the intentionality of interfaithful families—

in contrast to the usual case of interfaithless ones—has changed the minds of many who used to be hands-down against this sort of thing. You can't argue with parents who want their kids to engage with faith, albeit in ways that might approach an uncomfortable sort of blending that seemed inappropriate not long ago.

As we read these stories and listen to the professionals explain what they do, we respect what is being created in certain families that are fortunate enough to have two parents who are religiously literate and able to navigate difficult waters emotionally, as a dual-faith household. But we still have a personal bias. It seems difficult to live simultaneously as a Jew and Christian, or as either of those and a Muslim, or be theologically both Christian and Jewish (unless you are a Messianic Jew, which is institutionally Christian and not considered Jewish by the Jewish community). Like it or not, the tenets of our traditions simply don't always correspond, as Rachel and Jeremy demonstrate in their quiet battle over the Eucharist. How deep can dual-involvement as a family really go before creating a fractured religious life? We would rather raise Sima in a way that she can fully absorb one tradition. And perhaps our bias is the depth at which we live in that tradition.

Rabbi Steven Carr Reuben, author of multiple books on interfaith marriage[27] and a regular contributor to Interfaith Family.com, explains in one of his popular videos on the topic of dual-faith families: "Religious consistency encourages an emotional stability for kids. Raise them in one, the other, both, or neither religion, but be consistent." But as he continues he shows his cards as well: "Pick an identity for your child...a tradition in which to raise them. Of course, once they are adults they, like all of us, have the opportunity to choose an identity for themselves." Then Rabbi Reuben explains that it is possible to raise a child in a single religious tradition while ensuring the child develops tolerance of both, ideally of all, traditions and, of course, love and respect for his or her parents and extended families. He concludes, "Every child raised in an interfaith family on some level will still think 'I am both, for I am part of my mother and part of my father.'"

Concerns about division within the family or using religion as an emotional tool often keep couples from creating dual-faith children or households. It is precisely the potential for children *choosing* one parent over the other that they want to avoid. When Wendy and Ahmed met, for example, as graduate students through a mutual friend, they enjoyed being together and thought little about their religious differences. As the friendship blossomed, they then spent a lot of time considering how their Catholic and Muslim backgrounds could or couldn't be integrated into a life together, including the consideration of children. Ahmed felt they should raise the children as both, but Wendy disagreed, not wanting religion to have any potentially divisive role in the home. "I want us to present a united front," she told him. She suggested they raise their children with a Muslim identity, while being exposed to Catholicism through her.

When Michal and Wendy discussed their choice, which was essentially the same as ours, an interesting question arose for both of them. When the time comes, how do we all explain to our kids about the *other* religion? "What does it mean that mom or dad is Catholic?" they imagined their kids someday wondering. They decided a few things.

They would explain to their children that the other religious tradition is not wrong or less. It is a part of how Mom or Dad grew up and helped make them who they are. And the ideas and practices remain meaningful to them. And of course, likewise, Mom or Dad don't think either of those things ("wrong" or "bad") about Islam or Judaism, either. Yet as a family we have chosen to focus on one set of traditions, stories, and practices, and to form a relationship with a specific religious community, all of which we believe will help you become a great person and will enrich our family life.

Within each of us, there is an internal intellectual and emotional life as well as an external expression of that through practice. Only the former is present within a child really, which means that the early expressions of faith in practice depend on the intention of the parents. Choosing a baptism, bris, or naming for a newborn has an impact on the child, or at least it will have an impact *if* the parents then decide to follow up with meaningful religious engagement to the children and family.

To paraphrase the quotation from Eileen Smith's book, if a welcoming ceremony is all that happens, why bother? As a rabbi, Michal has had too many interactions with families who agonized over the decision to circumcise their sons, only to swallow hard, do the deed, throw a party, and stop there, simultaneously beginning the boy's Jewish life and ending his Jewish upbringing. The same thing happens with baptisms, only parents don't squirm as much about having their child sprinkled with water.

Children mirror us. They watch what we do in order to know what they are to do. Whether it is throwing a ball or praying *salat*, we say to our kids, "Do what I do," and that's how they learn. So even if the baptism is followed up with catechism, it still may not truly feel a part of their life if mom and dad are never seen closer to the church than the drop-off line out on the street. This is another aspect of the advice "be consistent."

At the end of the day, there are countless options for raising healthy children with or without religious identities, all of which can work. But how do we know when we are making the right decision? In our own interview with Rabbi Steven Carr Reuben, we asked him to go a little deeper with us about his suggestion about consistency and preference for raising children with primary religious identities. We close with his comments: "Just about anything can work if a couple is committed and clear about their intention. I have seen many different family configurations and most of the time the kids do fine. The most important element is a lack of conflict for the parents; if they are in agreement and content with their decisions about religious practice and identity, whatever choices they made, the family will do just fine."

MICHAL **I have often wondered what creates an adult with an interest in religion: Nature or nurture? Events that occur later in life? I am sure these are important, but I remain convinced there is a gene for spirituality.**

I was raised in a family of four daughters, all of whom had the same household experience and nearly the same religious education. My older sister did not learn Hebrew or have a bat mitzvah; that was my novel addition to the family plan, which the other two sisters followed.

And here I am, a rabbi, and a woman who has remained religiously engaged throughout her life, while none of my sisters pursued any religious activity beyond their education, which ended in high school. As I look at my extended family, primarily a slew of second cousins, there are glimmers of the spirituality gene, showing up without fail exactly once on each branch that sprouted on our family tree from my maternal grandmother and her sisters. One is a Judaica artist, another teaches Jewish meditation, the third is a Buddhist chaplain. I cannot help imagining that somewhere woven into what my family lovingly refers to as the "Darkovskia Strain," referring to my grandmother and great aunts' original Russian maiden name, was something that each of us four received and our siblings simply did not.

Yet it is unlikely that we could know when our children are young who the budding rabbis, deacons, or teachers of Islam might be, or which might have a life event that encourages them to explore the spiritual realms. So it seems that the more knowledge and sense of identity bestowed upon and integrated by a child, the better able they will be to access it later in life, sometimes much later, and the more authentic it will feel. While life may ultimately lead them down a different path than the one in which they were raised, as many spiritual leaders have been known to advise—if you are seeking God, look to your own heritage first.

PART IV

Re-creating the Future

Interfaith marriages are tougher to navigate than most, and more likely to fail. That's what experts tell us, as you will see in the chapters to come.

That is why we are here, figuring out how to do it better, more consciously, and with more spirit. The statistics of the past need not predict the future of interfaith coupling and family-making. "Mixed-up" does not have to mean confused. There are new and better ways to make our unions thrive.

Then there is the issue of creating community in which we might thrive, finding others who are like us, and recruiting allies who can support us. Interfaith is still about faith, and forging stronger bonds of faith within and outside of our relationships and families will help create a new landscape for religious life in the generations to come.

CHAPTER 11

Am I Ruining Your Life?

A half century ago, sociologist Albert Gordon predicted that interfaith marriages were three times more likely to end in divorce than same-faith ones. His data was soft, but the impact of his opinion was far-reaching.[28] Since then, another survey in 2001, involving 35,000 respondents, came to similar, alarming conclusions.[29] Apparently, we who are in serious interfaith relationships should be particularly worried.

Both of these statistics are reported by Naomi Schaeffer Riley, whose own study includes some interesting results on this issue.[30] Riley's primary finding is that both marital happiness and divorce rates are tied closely to the religious identities of the couples. For Catholics, for instance, neither measure seems to be affected by the religious status of their partner. Yet for evangelical Christians, intermarriage seems to result in a significant decrease in satisfaction and an increase in divorce rate. Imbedded in this contrast is the dynamic that the higher divorce rate for evangelical marriages is offset by lower rates for Catholic intermarriages. Other combinations fall in between these extremes.

So what might all of this mean? For one thing, Riley's data supports the assumption we made previously—that a conservative, somewhat exclusionary religious outlook, as found in many evangelical communities, can lead to difficulties in interfaith marriage. Beyond that, it is hard to say. All of this data does a good job of describing what has happened in the past; it is likely to describe the future to some extent, as well, but the data is not predictive and doesn't take into account which couples went into their marriages with better preparation and expectations. After all, in most cases, the majority of informed intermarried couples stay together in satisfying unions.

Given our professions, we knew before committing to each other that our union would create a unique set of personal challenges. This has never been so difficult as the disappointing experience we had with the congregation that loved Michal, saw her as the ideal rabbi for them, but wouldn't hire her because of who Jon is. They couldn't get their collective head around having a Catholic as the rabbi's husband, regardless of his obvious support for her work, his engagement with Judaism, and his general geniality in their midst, all of which they freely acknowledged.

"But he's not a Jew. What would people think?" a congregational board member wondered out loud. The committee responsible for the rabbinic search made every effort to assure us this man's concern represented only a small minority of the community. Then the phone call came some weeks later. "We're sorry. We won't be hiring you. It's about Jon."

There are many other congregations that would have the same concern, just as there are others that would consider us a model family. Well, lesson learned. We now know to have our family configuration clearly described before any significant conversations and interview trips take place.

A similar situation exists potentially for Jon, and he has already noticed a couple of opportunities with publishing houses that would not consider his candidacy should he apply. He hasn't been actively looking for a new job since we met, but it is always useful to see what piques your interest as positions arise. In his writing, as well, he has felt the change. Now, he's too "edgy" for some magazines and organizations he once wrote for. He remembers the day that he changed his author bio on the major websites where his writing frequently appears. That day, Jon was scared of what people would think. *But it is who I am*, he told himself, as he hit "Accept changes." In both of our cases, of course, what's the point of spending your life working with people who disapprove of you?

Unfortunately, external disapproval is an issue for many interfaith couples, coming not only from family members but employers, colleagues, and even friends, and it is always a source of stress. Some people consider potential disapproval from such quarters before they even make a decision to enter a serious relationship with someone of another faith. Depending on their relationships with family and the social and religious environments in which they live, even in the absence of their own concerns, such pressure can create a pretty tough situation.

As Wendy, a Catholic married to a Muslim, shared with us: "The times in our relationship when faith threatened to divide us, the root was often from the outside—either someone telling me that 'these things never work out,' or someone telling him that I will secretly not teach our children about Islam and take them away from him."

This type of external pressure was an up-close issue for Michal early on, as Jon's family struggled with her presence in his life. Eventually she understood that our relationship was just the *latest* symptom of Jon's deviation from the spiritual path of his upbringing, and that realization helped calm her emotional response during some difficult early exchanges. Then, as we described earlier, once everyone met one another there was an emotional connection, understanding, and even welcoming. Several years later, we now do a pretty good job of being together, enjoying activities, and engaging with each other personally and intellectually around the things we can share, while avoiding the topics that tend to divide us.

Other external pressures felt by Michal were caused not so much by our religious differences but by how others were experiencing the changes in Jon's life. What comes naturally to a person while making changes in his life for the better can sometimes still be jarring to loved ones nearby. Within a two-year span, Jon divorced, lost one hundred pounds, started dating Michal, and converted to Catholicism. So, when Jon introduced Michal to his kids about eighteen months after the original family had broken up, the kids felt it all as somehow too quick. All in all, probably too many changes at once. Jon experienced them as positive, but those who loved him needed more time.

We can experience these changes inside ourselves, finding a new path of life and joy, but the smiles on our faces are occasionally "lost" on the people around us looking in. That alone can cause stress, as none of us want our loved ones to be worrying about us. These external stresses that we experienced are fairly ordinary and may mirror some of your own. And often, they had nothing directly to do with what was going on in our religious lives. For example, Jon's change in diet and lifestyle had more impact on his relationship with his son than the conversion did; Joe missed bonding over pizzas or devouring bags of chips together while watching a ball game.

Today, the ways we struggle within our relationship also usually have little to do with religion, primarily because we are so similar as religious people, even if from different traditions. With religion such an active and overt part of our daily lives, it is rare that latent issues seem to stem from faith. Instead, our primary struggles are more classic personality clashes, some even boiling down to stereotypical male vs. female dynamics of thinking vs. feeling, or stating opinions vs. asking questions.

MICHAL There is one way in which religion kept erupting in our lives, only we didn't realize it at first. There was a

stretch of many weeks when Jon and I would intensely argue on Friday afternoons while cleaning and cooking in preparation for dinner guests, or to bring food to another home or to a Shabbat potluck lunch. Stress would build up in Jon, as we would be furiously busy with preparations, and we would begin to argue about something, almost anything really, and it didn't take long for it to get heated. As friends were about to ring our bell for dinner, or we were needing to walk out the door to go, it would still be unresolved and Jon would threaten to stay home or cancel our plans: "We aren't going out and making nice-nice with other people on Shabbat if in reality we are screaming at each other!" he'd say, or something similar. We never ended up actually abandoning plans, but we were late on a few occasions.

At least twice, good friends said, "How was your week?" and Jon responded, "Pretty good, but not today. Today, we've just been fighting like cats." We didn't realize *what* we were arguing about for a long time.

Finally, I noticed that the arguments were almost *only* happening on Fridays. I noted that to Jon, who then realized why. "It seems that we are always stressed and trying to do too much on Friday afternoon," he said, "and it doesn't seem like a good way to enter Shabbat. I don't want a day of rest if it means that I'm running around crazy for several hours every Friday afternoon."

"Really? That's interesting," I replied, "because it never feels like stress to me. It is just how Shabbat kind of works, especially if you have a job and don't have all day to prepare."

"The rushing around doesn't bother you?"

"I don't think so. Sometimes it feels a little chaotic, but I am pretty good at navigating it I think."

And while that was essentially the end of the eruptions, the situation in some ways points to what we think is the source of our biggest challenge as a couple. This, too, is not unusual: we've had to learn how to develop new ways of being in this new relationship and to communicate better.

Prior to meeting, we came from radically different situations, as opposite as our religious upbringings had been. Jon married at twenty-one and spent seventeen years in a mostly unhappy marriage, emotionally shutting down at times in order to remain in the relationship, keep his vow, and raise his children. Michal was single for most of her adult life and was used to being independent—personally, professionally, and financially. So neither of us had a strong track record of effectively sharing our lives when we met, and while we never doubted that the other was the person with whom we wanted to finally do just that, we weren't well equipped.

For Michal, it didn't take long for any conversation about doing some task or making a decision to feel like unnecessary negotiation and a diminishment of her capacity in some way. And Jon found that he was dealing with anger, a feeling to which he was not accustomed; he realized he hadn't allowed himself to be emotionally invested or vulnerable in his prior relationship and sometimes didn't know how to respond to feelings, or to Michal, in those moments.

But for other people we know, religion does indeed become a source of serious strife within a relationship. As Wendy wrote to us about her marriage to Ahmed: "I believe that when we fight, the chances of our fight reaching a deeper level are higher than perhaps couples from the same faith." Her words are both perceptive and wise: "It is in those moments of disagreement that we resort to our individual culture and faith, and become defensive and stubborn. It is almost like we use our faiths as shields, dividing us." They occasionally even resorted to accusing the other of trespasses of the extreme forms of their respective faiths, blaming the other for "archaic" Muslim inheritance laws or Catholic "superstitions." Surely these sorts of painful, private moments between a couple, when we say things that we would never imagine saying at calmer moments or in public, are also fed in subtle ways by the external messages we have received from others.

We point blank asked Laurie and Paula, a Lutheran and Buddhist who recently created a home together: "Are there ways in which you're ruining each other's lives?" Both responded, "Not at all." Laurie began, "On the contrary! Our relationship is an enormous enrichment for me. She helps me to affirm my own commitments. I have a hybrid sort of religious view now, yet it makes me more conscious of my own faith and tradition." And then Paula: "She may have actually *saved* my life. We were both in our mid-forties when we met, and having this relationship has been very good for both of us. Our relationship is an opportunity to come to understand myself better, and to wrestle in an honest way with what these differences are. I don't feel any push at all [from Laurie] to be something that I'm not, and I see it as an opportunity to see myself and the world."

We loved this idea of saving each other's lives. There are ways in which we, too, feel this way, especially in how we've taken each other to such a different place, regardless of the stressful growth it causes. After all, certain stress is good, and one person's stress may be another's growth. Jon can often feel to Michal like a rough surface that softens her edges, challenging her to find more flexibility in her own life. And Jon welcomes the emotional tone that Michal not only evokes, but demands, even if it is painful for both at times. All of this yin and yang is both religious and not, and it is good.

Another thing we have in common with Laurie and Paula that is different for many newer couples is our life stage. Being older and having been in previous marriages and relationships have both benefits and, as we have already described, challenges. We read often about the number of people who marry and divorce only to repeat their relationship failures over and over again. That is not our pattern, and we believe that a connection to religious life and community might contribute to receiving the insight, hearing the input, and seeking the assistance we need to move forward in our lives with emotional intelligence and self-knowledge.

Lately, people have been interested in what it is like for us to write a book together. Michal's standard response quickly became, "Well, let's just say our worship styles are more similar than our writing styles," which was usually accompanied by a suggestive smile. A couple of times, Jon frankly told close friends, "We fought all afternoon." Jon writes volumes on paper, expecting to edit later; Michal writes and refines in her head. Jon veers toward wanting to be affable, with extra narrative that feels welcoming and supportive; Michal's writing is more compact. Once we figured out these patterns, we learned to blend and integrate them. The struggles ceased and the work flowed back and forth between us more easily. The writing itself could have broken up our marriage (that subject certainly came up more than once on a Friday afternoon!), but instead, we worked it out and found how, in fact, we help each other.

CHAPTER 12

Finding and Creating Allies

Leslie and Jerry identified the primary challenge in their relationship. It is their sense of isolation, of loneliness, not as individuals, but as a couple. They don't know other couples like them living in their area who have similar religious commitments and values. Even supportive church and synagogue communities don't fill this need, as only one of them can fully inhabit their religious selves at those moments. "Find us a few couples we can study with, to explore and deepen our understanding of each other's traditions," Leslie implored us. We would have gladly joined them. We need allies as much as they, and you, do.

Many other couples we spoke with over the last year are experiencing a similar feeling of being alone. Sometimes their desire is to learn; other times it is to have a willing ear to process the choices they're making and the challenges they're facing. Often it is simply a relief to be able to share their lives with others who "get it" in some way. And the loneliness is not solely due to a lack of peers, but sometimes due to distance from family, lack of community, or feelings of "otherness" within the mainstream culture.

Personally, we have experienced this in an even more foundational place: We've felt isolated by not having enough connections with people with whom we can share progressive values as well as active, religious lives. This is because our religious practice tends to be too traditional for most liberals, and yet our values tend to be too liberal for those with orthodox or conservative religious commitments. As a result, we are sometimes left feeling stuck in a strange middle.

We spend a fair amount of time seeking others with whom we can share what is important to us. These allies need not be couples or families, nor interfaith, just religiously interested and engaged, and willing to spend time praying or studying or discussing or practicing a way of being that makes more room for God in the world.

One obvious place to look for allies on your religious journey is established institutions. There are plenty of congregations, now, that are geared to not just acceptance of interfaith couples, but cultivation of them. They offer classes to educate partners who are newer to the faith and its traditions; they are welcoming of the non-Christian, non-Muslim, non-Hindu partner in appropriate ritual events; they take an inclusive "under the wing" approach to including everyone who is present and interested in participating. And of course, the specifically interfaith organizations and schools already mentioned can provide a great place to start. If this is not available in your city or not accessible in your community, social media provides lots of avenues to start a group of your own, even just for socialization. Yes, it takes some effort, but so does fulfilling religious life in general.

Perhaps a unique aspect of interfaith relationships in the 21st century is that some have reached the second generation. There are now adults who grew up in active interfaith families. They are themselves getting married. They are having kids of their own. What a challenge this presents to institutions that have not yet begun to find a full place for interfaith families in their rituals, life-cycle events, or midst.

Rabbi Ike Serotta talked about this with us. In answer to the question, *How has interfaith marriage changed in your congregation?* he replied, "I'm now facing the grown children of interfaith marriages who are getting married. They are one hundred percent identified as Jews, and now marrying non-Jews themselves. It presents a different question for the rabbi than we faced a generation ago. I realize they have a good role model of how an interfaith marriage can affirm Judaism." In other words, Ike went on to say, "Who am I to tell them that it can't be done?"

There is a persistent sense that if one faith (or congregation) does not welcome the new kind of couple, then another will. And—as we've said—arguing with the existence of interfaith marriage is like yelling at the ocean because you don't appreciate the tides. So, when we asked what Rabbi Ike's motivations were in working overtime to reach out to interfaith couples, even in ways that he does not yet fully understand himself, he said: "I want the synagogue to be welcoming—not just the church." His concern mirrors a common perception in the religious world, that Jewish institutions *are* in fact less welcoming to inter- and multi-faith families. This is, indeed, why organizations like Interfaith Family.com exist. When Michal and Rabbi Ike compared notes they agreed that finding more ways to say "yes," or at least to be in conversation with a couple or family, would be helpful. Even if he knows that he can't, or won't, perform a wedding, a rabbi who speaks to a couple and offers a referral or other suggestion keeps doors open that can otherwise close quickly.

But it's not just institutions and clergy that have work to do. In fact, we believe that interfaith couples themselves need to do more work if they want more understanding. That is one of the primary motivations we had in writing this book: to encourage you to think, reflect, talk, get some counseling—not to simply assume that it will all work out fine. That way, when you are confronted by skeptical family and friends you can present a clear vision of what you're hoping for in your lives together, religiously and otherwise, and you can recruit their support through real conversation and respectful consideration. It doesn't mean you will agree, but you will better understand each other and bring them into your relationship in a way that simply ignoring them never will.

We also believe that interfaith couples and families need to be respectful in what we ask of our churches, synagogues, mosques, temples, and their clergy. We should show that we honor the religious traditions that are bending in new ways to accommodate the changes that our family constellations prompt, instead of being perceived as always pushing every boundary. This happened to Michal when a couple inquired as to whether she will officiate their wedding...at 11:30 on a Saturday morning. "Our rabbi isn't available," they explained via e-mail. "Really?" she said to Jon upon reading the request, *"Really?! Do you think that maybe that's because he is still leading a bar mitzvah that Shabbat morning, or leading his congregation in a Torah discussion?"* Her e-mail response was more kindly worded than that, but you get the idea. There is no reason why an interfaith marriage needs to contradict core principles of any faith. "Unfortunately," as Michal heard from a local cantor who's a good friend of our family, "clergy are mostly seen as just another vendor to couples getting married." Frankly, if a couple plans no connection to religious community we would rather see them married by a judge than ask clergy to violate their principles, or find the clergy who make their money by doing just that. We would rather see more couples make an effort to respect those who are trying to find new ways to welcome us into worship, ritual, and practice.

As we think finally about how to move forward in our collective lives we again picture the concentric circles that were part of our own marriage ceremony. Through thoughtful reflection and discussion we can hold those closest rings of family and dear ones close. And more and more we can find community, who make up the next ring of circles around us, with whom we can share our faith journeys, life-cycle events, and personal milestones, within and beyond traditional faith institutions. Many progressive churches, synagogues, and, increasingly, mosques welcome us in our many configurations. Then, interfaith organizations such as those in Chicago and Washington, D.C., create unique communities that share a specific approach to integrating religious traditions. And social media create new options for reaching out and finding allies, confidantes, and study partners.

Meanwhile, that centermost of circles is still the two of you, and perhaps your children. It is important to ask the difficult questions, and the answers are not always straightforward. Establishing what is important to you, what values will guide your lives together, the significance of your religious tradition and practice, and what you will teach your children is vital on the front end. There are many questions and so many possibilities for creating lives full of spiritual meaning and practice in the world. With effort, perhaps a lot of effort, you will discover the path that can work for you.

There is no single answer to know that you are on the correct path. But we remember the words of one of the experts we interviewed. It was Jane Kaplan who reflected on scores of interviews she conducted a decade ago for the book she wrote on interfaith marriages. She recalled coming to a single conclusion: "It seems that truly any choice a couple makes can work, or can *not work*. It will work when the couple is on board together, when they are clear with each other, and when they are committed to the decisions they've made."

Epilogue

[IM chat between Jon and Michal on the day we finished the final manuscript for *Mixed-Up Love*]

MICHAL: Hey hun, to paraphrase Sima's current favorite phrase: *"We* did it!"

JON: Ha! Okay, how?

MICHAL: How...what?

JON: How did we make a relationship work? How did we write the book?

MICHAL: Good questions, what do you think?

JON: I don't think we can say, clearly, yet, how we made a relationship work. I think we can only say what we have done thus far, or what decisions and values are guiding what we do. What works and what doesn't.

MICHAL: I think we have said that pretty clearly.

JON: I agree.

MICHAL: So I think we just wrote a book—or at least a draft of one.

JON: Maybe instead: WHY we wrote a book. Why did we?

MICHAL: Well, I think you will disagree on this. I think it is because it is your next chapter of what you had already written.

JON: You are right, I disagree, because I never would have written a book for that reason. Definitely not in this case. It isn't about me.

MICHAL: No, it isn't about you, but you definitely had the passion to write about religious identity and this was a great vehicle to do that in a concrete way.

JON: That's true. And I DO have that passion. I think that is important because I think people hear discussion about it and say to themselves, that's me too!

MICHAL: Or maybe because we are so OUT about it while we are immersed in so many religious worlds.

JON: Yes. There may have been a bit of coming out of the closet in writing the book.

MICHAL: Well, I suspect we will begin to hear a lot of "me too" in the coming months.

JON: I would love to hear a lot of that. In fact, it wouldn't be unusual to put an email address in the closing chapter, saying: contact us.

MICHAL: I am just glad our marriage survived it.

JON: I agree. The marriage almost didn't survive it.

MICHAL: That might be a little strong.

JON: But I suspect that that is part of the nature of the complexity of the book and the way that the book is such a part of our life. In other words, the book is not just something extra that we did to have fun, or to make money, or because we have big egos. The book comes right from who we are, both together and separately. To deal with that intimate of stuff day after day is to claw at each other's souls.

MICHAL: But that isn't why it was hard, because content was easy. I think I needed to become a full partner as an author since you are a publishing professional.

JON: Maybe that's true. But my version sounded more poignant...

MICHAL: We certainly got to work out a lot of other stuff.

JON: Writing the book, though, DID cause us to rethink and continue to think about certain really important things, like, how much we give of ourselves and of our time (not enough).

MICHAL: Yes, I feel newly radicalized. We both tend in that direction. Harder to make huge shifts now though with a toddler and 2 kids in college.

JON: It is almost like, now that the book is written, we need to get our butts out there and do more.

MICHAL: I agree. And I hope we recruit good company to join us.

JON: That could be how we conclude the epilogue.

MICHAL: I think we just did.

Notes

1. This Georgetown survey is available at http://cara.georgetown.edu/MarriageReport.pdf.

2. The most extreme version of this can be seen in the book, and accompanying website, http://preventintermarriage.com.

3. See, for instance, Sylvia Barack Fishman's *Double or Nothing? Jewish Families and Mixed Marriage* (Hanover, NH: Brandeis University Press, 2004); Jane Kaplan's *Interfaith Families: Personal Stories of Jewish-Christian Intermarriage* (Westport, CT: Praeger, 2004); and Naomi Schaefer Riley's *'Til Faith Do Us Part: How Interfaith Marriage Is Transforming America* (New York: Oxford University Press, 2013).

4. Karen Armstrong, *Islam: A Short History* (New York: Modern Library, 2002), ix.

5. Sylvia Boorstein, *That's Funny, You Don't Look Buddhist: On Being a Faithful Jew and a Passionate Buddhist* (San Francisco: HarperSanFrancisco, 1997).

6. Paul F. Knitter, *Without Buddha I Could Not Be a Christian*, 2nd ed. (New York: OneWorld Publications, 2013). More recently, Knitter uses what he calls an "inappropriate analogy" for his own spiritual self by comparing it to "A 'Hypostatic Union' of Two Practices but One Person." You may want to read his article with that title in the journal *Buddhist-Christian Studies* 32 (2012): 19–26.

7. Susan Katz Miller, *Being Both: Embracing Two Religions in One Interfaith Family* (Boston: Beacon Press, 2013).

8. Joshua Harris, *I Kissed Dating Goodbye* (Sisters, OR: Multnomah Books, 1997).

9. Lauren F. Winner, "The Countercultural Path," in *5 Paths to the Love of Your Life: Defining Your Dating Style* (Colorado Springs, CO: NavPress, 2005), 17–56.

Notes

10. Listen to Matt Chandler's sermon on this topic, available on YouTube as of this writing at http://www.youtube.com/watch?v=3BiiKx3Lr_o; and Mark Driscoll's at https://www.youtube.com/watch?v=8evyJXMBiE8, among others.

11. As of April 25, 2013. www.winninghimwithoutwords.com.

12. Jane Kaplan, *Interfaith Families: Personal Stories of Jewish-Christian Intermarriage* (Westport, CT: Praeger, 2004).

13. Melissa Kite, "Till Faith Do Us Part," *The Spectator*, October 13, 2012, 14.

14. For example, a 2007 survey of young Catholics done by the Center for Applied Research in the Apostolate at Georgetown University found that, among those who had never married, only 7 percent responded that it was "very important" to wed someone who was also Catholic. This survey is available at http://cara.georgetown.edu/MarriageReport.pdf.

15. Andrew MacBeth, *Dearly Beloved: Navigating Your Church Wedding* (New York: Seabury, 2007), 87.

16. BBC Asian Network, July 5, 2012; http://www.youtube.com/watch?v=Btx5Rek2tns.

17. Joshua Eli Plaut, *A Kosher Christmas: 'Tis the Season to Be Jewish* (New Brunswick, NJ: Rutgers University Press, 2012).

18. Thomas Fuller, "Monks Lose Relevance as Thailand Grows Richer," *New York Times*, December 18, 2012. Available at http://www.nytimes.com/2012/12/19/world/asia/thai-buddhist-monks-struggle-to-stay-relevant.html.

19. Nathan Englander, "Reb Kringle," in *For the Relief of Unbearable Urges* (New York: Vintage International, 2000), 139–152.

20. Huma Qureshi, "How Do Muslims Celebrate Christmas? Turkey, Top of the Pops and Shloer," *The Guardian* (London), December 19, 2012. Available at http://www.guardian.co.uk/commentisfree/belief/2012/dec/19/muslims-celebrate-christmas-turkey-top-pops.

21. See Wayne Muller's *Sabbath: Finding Rest, Renewal, and Delight in Our Daily Lives* (New York: Bantam, 2000); and MaryAnn McKibben Dana's *Sabbath in the Suburbs: A Family's Experiment with Holy Time* (St. Louis: Chalice Press, 2012).

22. See, for instance, National Religious Partnership for the Environment, www.nrpe.org; and Islamic Foundation for Ecology and Environmental Sciences, http://fore.research.yale.edu/religion/islam/projects/islamic_foundation.html.

23. Naomi Schaefer Riley, *'Til Faith Do Us Part,* 130.

24. http://www.iffp.net. A book has just been published out of the experience of one family in IFFP: See Susan Katz Miller's *Being Both: Embracing Two Religions in One Interfaith Family* (Boston: Beacon Press, 2013).

25. In traditional communities, *rebbetzin* is the name often given to the rabbi's wife. It is a transliterated Yiddish word that's roughly equivalent to "rebbe's female," like the "pastor's wife" in Christian traditions. In progressive communities, we use the word *rebbetzman*, instead, as a tongue-in-cheek equivalent for guys like Jon.

26. Eileen O'Farrell Smith, *Making Our Way to Shore: A Celebration of Hebrew Naming and Baptism.* Virtualbookworm.com, 2004, 3.

27. See, for instance, Steven Carr Reuben's *There's an Easter Egg on Your Seder Plate: Surviving Your Child's Interfaith Marriage* (Santa Barbara, CA: Praeger, 2007); and *But How Will You Raise the Children? A Guide to Interfaith Marriage* (New York: Pocket Books, 1987).

28. Albert I. Gordon, *Intermarriage: Interfaith, Interracial, Interethnic* (Boston: Beacon Press, 1964), 346–348. In the spring of 1967, for example, Virginia's Assistant Attorney General used this book as "expert opinion" before the U.S. Supreme Court to justify Virginia's ban on interracial marriages. The Commonwealth of Virginia lost, and Mildred and Richard Loving won, in this landmark case for civil rights in America.

29. This is the 2001 American Religious Identification Survey, as noted on page 123 of Naomi Schaefer Riley's chapter "Interfaith Divorce" in *'Til Faith Do Us Part.*

30. Naomi Schaefer Riley's chapter "Interfaith Divorce" in *'Til Faith Do Us Part.*

Acknowledgments

This book has been, by definition, collaborative. From day one, we have been reading, researching, questioning, thinking, and writing as a couple. Also from the start, we've been talking with and learning from others. We are grateful to the many people who shared their personal lives, professional expertise, or both, with us.

We turned to our friend Karen Kushner, educational consultant to InterfaithFamily.com, to get us started as we began to approach the issues we wished to include in this book. Her broad experience and expertise helped frame the issues and topics that would form the core of the work.

Local clergy and other colleagues candidly shared their own experiences and advice. Thanks especially to Dr. Phil Amerson, Rev. Andy MacBeth, Rabbi Ari Moffic, Father Robert Oldershaw, Rabbi Steven Carr Reuben, and Rabbi Isaac Serotta.

Thanks to Eboo Patel, Jane Kaplan, Jim Rooney, and Jack Learmonth for sharing their experiences in the interfaith world and helping us connect with some of the couples and families that appear in this book.

Dr. Gerald Postema and Leslie Winner graciously shared their experiences, which are shared openly in this book.

And then there are the dozens of you that appear incognito. Our story would hardly stand without yours beside it. Our heartfelt thanks are extended equally to all of you.

We are grateful to our parents and siblings for the various ways they either put up with, or embrace, us as an interfaith family. Michal's parents, Maurice and Aviva Woll, have been particularly supportive throughout this process, and we have enjoyed our frequent conversations with them around the book and appreciate their agreement to being teased publicly.

Thank you and much love, also, to Clelia and Joseph, our two terrific, now-suddenly-adult kids. We are enjoying watching you both grow into who you are and even, dare we say, discovering your own spiritual identities.

Thank you to our publisher, Wendy Grisham, and Chelsea Apple, her editorial assistant, for their encouragement and guidance. And Greg Daniel is, as always, both a great agent and friend.

A final word about the two extraordinary women to whom we have dedicated this book: Susie Learmonth and Jane Curtis embraced us immediately, both individually and as a couple, shared our mutual interests in religious thought and identity, and surrounded us in our early Vermont years with kindnesses and love that we will cherish forever.

And then there is Sima, our joyous treasure. She puts up with us, too.

About the Authors

JON M. SWEENEY is an independent scholar, culture critic, and popular speaker with twenty-five years of experience in spirituality trade publishing. For many years, he was the vice president of marketing for Jewish Lights Publishing and cofounder of SkyLight Paths Publishing, a multi-faith trade book publisher in Vermont. Since 2004, he has been editor-in-chief at Paraclete Press in Massachusetts. Jon is the author or editor of twenty books focusing on popular medieval history and spiritual memoir including *The Pope Who Quit: A True Medieval Tale of Mystery, Death, and Salvation*, a History Book Club selection that was recently optioned by HBO, Inc., and *Francis of Assisi in His Own Words: The Essential Writings*. Raised an evangelical Protestant, today Jon is a Catholic who prefers a monastic-style practice.

MICHAL WOLL is a gifted rabbi, liturgist, pastoral counselor, physical therapist, and yogi with twenty-five years of experience and three advanced degrees. After graduating from Northwestern University and MIT with degrees in bioengineering, she worked in the medical device industry developing dialysis and burn care products. There she discovered a passion for medical ethics and quality of life issues, eventually turning to clinical medicine and chaplaincy. She is a graduate of the Reconstructionist Rabbinical College in Philadelphia and currently serves as rabbi of the Ann Arbor Reconstructionist Congregation. Michal has passion for teaching and creating ritual and deep appreciation of Judaism as both a communal identity and a transformative, spiritual path.

Jon and Michal live in Ann Arbor, Michigan, and are raising their daughter Sima in a Jewish home. You can contact them at mixeduplove.thebook@gmail.com.